TEACHER'S PET PUBLICATIONS

PUZZLE PACK
for
A Midsummer Night's Dream

based on the play by
William Shakespeare

Written by
William T. Collins

© 2005 Teacher's Pet Publications
All Rights Reserved

The materials in this packet are copyrighted
by Teacher's Pet Publications, Inc.

These pages may be duplicated by the purchaser
for use in the purchaser's own classroom.

Copying any of these materials and distributing them
for any other purpose is a violation of the copyright laws.

© 2005 Teacher's Pet Publications, Inc.
www.tpet.com

INTRODUCTION
If you already own the LitPlan for this title, this Puzzle Pack will refresh your Unit Resource Materials and Vocabulary Resource Materials sections plus give you additional materials you can substitute into the tests. If you do not already have a complete LitPlan, these pages will give you some supplemental materials to use with your own plan. There are two main groups of materials: one set for unit words (such as characters' names, symbols, places, etc.) and one set for vocabulary words associated with the book.

WORD LIST
There is a word list for both the unit words and the vocabulary words. These lists show you which words are being used in the materials and the clues or definitions being used for those words. You may want to give students a word list with clues/definitions to help them, or you may want students to only have a word list (without clues/definitions) if you want them to work a little harder. Both are available for duplication. The word lists can also be your "calling key" for the bingo games.

FILL IN THE BLANK AND MATCHING
There are 4 each of the fill in the blank and matching worksheets for both the unit and vocabulary words. These pages can be used either as extra worksheets for students or as objective parts of a unit test. They can be done individually if students need extra help or as a whole class activity to review the material covered.

MAGIC SQUARES
The magic squares not only reinforce the material covered but also work on reasoning and math skills. Many teachers have told us that their students really enjoy doing these!

WORD SEARCH PUZZLES
The word search words go in all directions, as indicated on your answer keys. Two of the word search puzzles have the clues listed rather than the words. This makes the puzzle a little more difficult, but it reinforces the material better. Two word search puzzles have words only for students who find the clue puzzles too difficult.

CROSSWORD PUZZLES
Both unit and vocabulary word sections have 4 crossword puzzles.

BINGO CARDS
There are 32 individual bingo cards for the unit words and 32 individual bingo cards for the vocabulary words. You can use your word list as a "call list," calling the words at random and marking them off of your list as you go, or you could use the flash cards by cutting them apart and drawing the words at random from a hat (or box or whatever). To make a better review, you might ask for the definition and spelling of each word as you call it out–or you could call out the definitions and have students tell you the words they need to look for on the puzzle.

JUGGLE LETTERS
The vocabulary juggle letter game is intended to help students learn the spellings of the words. One sheet has the definitions listed on it as an extra help for students who need it or to reinforce the definitions if you choose to do so.

FLASH CARDS
We've included a set of vocabulary flash cards you can duplicate, cut, and fold for your students. Some teachers make a few sets for general use by the class; others make a set for each student. Some teachers duplicate them for each student and have the students cut & fold their own. You can cut out just the words and put them in a hat, have each student pick out one word and write the definition and a sentence for that word. Students then swap words and papers, with the next student adding a sentence of his own under the last one. You can have students swap as many times as you like. Each time the student will read the sentences written prior to his own and then add a sentence. You can cut out the words and definitions separately and play "I Have; Who Has?" Each student in the room draws a word and definition. The first student says, "I have (the name of the word). Who has the definition?" The student with the definition reads it then says, "I have (the name of the vocabulary word she has). Who has the definition?" The round continues until all words and definitions have been given.

Midsummer Night's Dream Word List

No.	Word	Clue/Definition
1.	ACT	Play division
2.	ASS	Puck changes Bottom's head to that of an ___.
3.	BOTTOM	Wants to play all the roles
4.	DEMETRIUS	Helena loves him, but he is to marry Hermia.
5.	DREAM	A Midsummer Night's ___
6.	EGEUS	Father of Hermia
7.	EYES	Oberon commands Puck to anoint Demetrius's ___ as he sleeps.
8.	FLOWER	Oberon sends Puck to find one struck by Cupid's arrow.
9.	FLUTE	Plays Thisby
10.	HELENA	Tells Hermia's plans to Demetrius
11.	HERMIA	Arranges to meet Lysander in the woods
12.	HIPPOLYTA	Queen of the Amazons
13.	JUDGEMENT	'Your eyes must look with his ___.'
14.	LOVE	Feeling Helena has for Demetrius
15.	LYSANDER	Hermia loves him.
16.	MIDSUMMER	A ___ Night's Dream
17.	NUN	Hermia will have to live as one if she refuses to marry Demetrius.
18.	OBERON	King of the Fairies
19.	PROLOGUE	Bottom wants one written for the play.
20.	PUCK	Robin Goodfellow
21.	QUINCE	Writes 'Pyramus and Thisby'
22.	SCENE	Act division
23.	SHAKESPEARE	Author of MND
24.	SNOUT	Plays Wall
25.	SNUG	Plays Lion
26.	STAGE	Where plays are performed
27.	THESEUS	Duke of Athens
28.	TITANIA	Queen of the Fairies
29.	WALL	What P & T talked through
30.	WEDDING	Topic Theseus and Hippolyta discuss at play's start
31.	WOODS	Where Lysander & Hermia agree to meet

Midsummer Night's Dream Fill In The Blanks 1

_____ 1. Where Lysander & Hermia agree to meet

_____ 2. Oberon sends Puck to find one struck by Cupid's arrow.

_____ 3. Where plays are performed

_____ 4. Puck changes Bottom's head to that of an ___.

_____ 5. Plays Wall

_____ 6. Tells Hermia's plans to Demetrius

_____ 7. Helena loves him, but he is to marry Hermia.

_____ 8. 'Your eyes must look with his ___.'

_____ 9. Play division

_____ 10. Queen of the Fairies

_____ 11. Hermia loves him.

_____ 12. Oberon commands Puck to anoint Demetrius's ___ as he sleeps.

_____ 13. Robin Goodfellow

_____ 14. Wants to play all the roles

_____ 15. A ___ Night's Dream

_____ 16. Plays Lion

_____ 17. A Midsummer Night's ___

_____ 18. Act division

_____ 19. Plays Thisby

_____ 20. Father of Hermia

Midsummer Night's Dream Fill In The Blanks 1 Answer Key

WOODS	1. Where Lysander & Hermia agree to meet
FLOWER	2. Oberon sends Puck to find one struck by Cupid's arrow.
STAGE	3. Where plays are performed
ASS	4. Puck changes Bottom's head to that of an ___.
SNOUT	5. Plays Wall
HELENA	6. Tells Hermia's plans to Demetrius
DEMETRIUS	7. Helena loves him, but he is to marry Hermia.
JUDGEMENT	8. 'Your eyes must look with his ___.'
ACT	9. Play division
TITANIA	10. Queen of the Fairies
LYSANDER	11. Hermia loves him.
EYES	12. Oberon commands Puck to anoint Demetrius's ___ as he sleeps.
PUCK	13. Robin Goodfellow
BOTTOM	14. Wants to play all the roles
MIDSUMMER	15. A ___ Night's Dream
SNUG	16. Plays Lion
DREAM	17. A Midsummer Night's ___
SCENE	18. Act division
FLUTE	19. Plays Thisby
EGEUS	20. Father of Hermia

Midsummer Night's Dream Fill In The Blanks 2

_____ 1. Play division

_____ 2. Plays Thisby

_____ 3. Duke of Athens

_____ 4. What P & T talked through

_____ 5. Robin Goodfellow

_____ 6. A Midsummer Night's ___

_____ 7. Queen of the Fairies

_____ 8. Hermia will have to live as one if she refuses to marry Demetrius.
_____ 9. Feeling Helena has for Demetrius

_____ 10. A ___ Night's Dream

_____ 11. Writes 'Pyramus and Thisby'

_____ 12. Bottom wants one written for the play.

_____ 13. Plays Lion

_____ 14. Act division

_____ 15. Helena loves him, but he is to marry Hermia.

_____ 16. Arranges to meet Lysander in the woods

_____ 17. Plays Wall

_____ 18. 'Your eyes must look with his ___.'

_____ 19. Father of Hermia

_____ 20. King of the Fairies

Midsummer Night's Dream Fill In The Blanks 2 Answer Key

ACT	1. Play division
FLUTE	2. Plays Thisby
THESEUS	3. Duke of Athens
WALL	4. What P & T talked through
PUCK	5. Robin Goodfellow
DREAM	6. A Midsummer Night's ___
TITANIA	7. Queen of the Fairies
NUN	8. Hermia will have to live as one if she refuses to marry Demetrius.
LOVE	9. Feeling Helena has for Demetrius
MIDSUMMER	10. A ___ Night's Dream
QUINCE	11. Writes 'Pyramus and Thisby'
PROLOGUE	12. Bottom wants one written for the play.
SNUG	13. Plays Lion
SCENE	14. Act division
DEMETRIUS	15. Helena loves him, but he is to marry Hermia.
HERMIA	16. Arranges to meet Lysander in the woods
SNOUT	17. Plays Wall
JUDGEMENT	18. 'Your eyes must look with his ___.'
EGEUS	19. Father of Hermia
OBERON	20. King of the Fairies

Midsummer Night's Dream Fill In The Blanks 3

_____
_____
_____
_____
_____
_____
_____
_____
_____
_____
_____
_____
_____
_____
_____
_____
_____
_____
_____
_____

1. Topic Theseus and Hippolyta discuss at play's start
2. Duke of Athens
3. Queen of the Amazons
4. What P & T talked through
5. Play division
6. Feeling Helena has for Demetrius
7. Where plays are performed
8. A ___ Night's Dream
9. Father of Hermia
10. Robin Goodfellow
11. Wants to play all the roles
12. Hermia loves him.
13. Plays Lion
14. Where Lysander & Hermia agree to meet
15. King of the Fairies
16. Arranges to meet Lysander in the woods
17. Plays Wall
18. Oberon commands Puck to anoint Demetrius's ___ as he sleeps.
19. Queen of the Fairies
20. Author of MND

Midsummer Night's Dream Fill In The Blanks 3 Answer Key

Answer	Clue
WEDDING	1. Topic Theseus and Hippolyta discuss at play's start
THESEUS	2. Duke of Athens
HIPPOLYTA	3. Queen of the Amazons
WALL	4. What P & T talked through
ACT	5. Play division
LOVE	6. Feeling Helena has for Demetrius
STAGE	7. Where plays are performed
MIDSUMMER	8. A ___ Night's Dream
EGEUS	9. Father of Hermia
PUCK	10. Robin Goodfellow
BOTTOM	11. Wants to play all the roles
LYSANDER	12. Hermia loves him.
SNUG	13. Plays Lion
WOODS	14. Where Lysander & Hermia agree to meet
OBERON	15. King of the Fairies
HERMIA	16. Arranges to meet Lysander in the woods
SNOUT	17. Plays Wall
EYES	18. Oberon commands Puck to anoint Demetrius's ___ as he sleeps.
TITANIA	19. Queen of the Fairies
SHAKESPEARE	20. Author of MND

Midsummer Night's Dream Fill In The Blanks 4

_____   1. Author of MND

_____   2. Oberon commands Puck to anoint Demetrius's ___ as he sleeps.

_____   3. Hermia will have to live as one if she refuses to marry Demetrius.

_____   4. Hermia loves him.

_____   5. King of the Fairies

_____   6. Tells Hermia's plans to Demetrius

_____   7. Wants to play all the roles

_____   8. Where Lysander & Hermia agree to meet

_____   9. A Midsummer Night's ___

_____   10. Robin Goodfellow

_____   11. Play division

_____   12. Writes 'Pyramus and Thisby'

_____   13. Feeling Helena has for Demetrius

_____   14. Plays Thisby

_____   15. What P & T talked through

_____   16. 'Your eyes must look with his ___.'

_____   17. Helena loves him, but he is to marry Hermia.

_____   18. Bottom wants one written for the play.

_____   19. Topic Theseus and Hippolyta discuss at play's start

_____   20. Queen of the Fairies

Midsummer Night's Dream Fill In The Blanks 4 Answer Key

SHAKESPEARE	1. Author of MND
EYES	2. Oberon commands Puck to anoint Demetrius's ___ as he sleeps.
NUN	3. Hermia will have to live as one if she refuses to marry Demetrius.
LYSANDER	4. Hermia loves him.
OBERON	5. King of the Fairies
HELENA	6. Tells Hermia's plans to Demetrius
BOTTOM	7. Wants to play all the roles
WOODS	8. Where Lysander & Hermia agree to meet
DREAM	9. A Midsummer Night's ___
PUCK	10. Robin Goodfellow
ACT	11. Play division
QUINCE	12. Writes 'Pyramus and Thisby'
LOVE	13. Feeling Helena has for Demetrius
FLUTE	14. Plays Thisby
WALL	15. What P & T talked through
JUDGEMENT	16. 'Your eyes must look with his ___.'
DEMETRIUS	17. Helena loves him, but he is to marry Hermia.
PROLOGUE	18. Bottom wants one written for the play.
WEDDING	19. Topic Theseus and Hippolyta discuss at play's start
TITANIA	20. Queen of the Fairies

Midsummer Night's Dream Matching 1

___ 1. PROLOGUE   A. Wants to play all the roles
___ 2. WOODS   B. A ___ Night's Dream
___ 3. SNOUT   C. Tells Hermia's plans to Demetrius
___ 4. STAGE   D. Arranges to meet Lysander in the woods
___ 5. NUN   E. What P & T talked through
___ 6. FLOWER   F. Father of Hermia
___ 7. SCENE   G. Writes 'Pyramus and Thisby'
___ 8. BOTTOM   H. Hermia loves him.
___ 9. LOVE   I. Plays Lion
___ 10. WALL   J. Bottom wants one written for the play.
___ 11. ASS   K. Robin Goodfellow
___ 12. DREAM   L. Hermia will have to live as one if she refuses to marry Demetrius.
___ 13. QUINCE   M. Puck changes Bottom's head to that of an ___.
___ 14. FLUTE   N. King of the Fairies
___ 15. WEDDING   O. Where Lysander & Hermia agree to meet
___ 16. PUCK   P. Play division
___ 17. EGEUS   Q. Plays Wall
___ 18. MIDSUMMER   R. Author of MND
___ 19. HELENA   S. A Midsummer Night's ___
___ 20. HERMIA   T. Act division
___ 21. SNUG   U. Topic Theseus and Hippolyta discuss at play's start
___ 22. LYSANDER   V. Feeling Helena has for Demetrius
___ 23. ACT   W. Oberon sends Puck to find one struck by Cupid's arrow.
___ 24. OBERON   X. Where plays are performed
___ 25. SHAKESPEARE   Y. Plays Thisby

Midsummer Night's Dream Matching 1 Answer Key

J - 1. PROLOGUE	A. Wants to play all the roles
O - 2. WOODS	B. A ___ Night's Dream
Q - 3. SNOUT	C. Tells Hermia's plans to Demetrius
X - 4. STAGE	D. Arranges to meet Lysander in the woods
L - 5. NUN	E. What P & T talked through
W - 6. FLOWER	F. Father of Hermia
T - 7. SCENE	G. Writes 'Pyramus and Thisby'
A - 8. BOTTOM	H. Hermia loves him.
V - 9. LOVE	I. Plays Lion
E - 10. WALL	J. Bottom wants one written for the play.
M - 11. ASS	K. Robin Goodfellow
S - 12. DREAM	L. Hermia will have to live as one if she refuses to marry Demetrius.
G - 13. QUINCE	M. Puck changes Bottom's head to that of an ___.
Y - 14. FLUTE	N. King of the Fairies
U - 15. WEDDING	O. Where Lysander & Hermia agree to meet
K - 16. PUCK	P. Play division
F - 17. EGEUS	Q. Plays Wall
B - 18. MIDSUMMER	R. Author of MND
C - 19. HELENA	S. A Midsummer Night's ___
D - 20. HERMIA	T. Act division
I - 21. SNUG	U. Topic Theseus and Hippolyta discuss at play's start
H - 22. LYSANDER	V. Feeling Helena has for Demetrius
P - 23. ACT	W. Oberon sends Puck to find one struck by Cupid's arrow.
N - 24. OBERON	X. Where plays are performed
R - 25. SHAKESPEARE	Y. Plays Thisby

Copyrighted

Midsummer Night's Dream Matching 2

___ 1. FLOWER
___ 2. QUINCE
___ 3. DREAM
___ 4. EYES
___ 5. WOODS
___ 6. STAGE
___ 7. PUCK
___ 8. ACT
___ 9. EGEUS
___ 10. TITANIA
___ 11. OBERON
___ 12. WEDDING
___ 13. HIPPOLYTA
___ 14. HERMIA
___ 15. JUDGEMENT
___ 16. HELENA
___ 17. WALL
___ 18. ASS
___ 19. SNUG
___ 20. MIDSUMMER
___ 21. FLUTE
___ 22. BOTTOM
___ 23. NUN
___ 24. PROLOGUE
___ 25. THESEUS

A. Writes 'Pyramus and Thisby'
B. 'Your eyes must look with his ___.'
C. Where plays are performed
D. Arranges to meet Lysander in the woods
E. Where Lysander & Hermia agree to meet
F. Play division
G. Queen of the Fairies
H. King of the Fairies
I. Hermia will have to live as one if she refuses to marry Demetrius.
J. Bottom wants one written for the play.
K. Topic Theseus and Hippolyta discuss at play's start
L. Duke of Athens
M. Plays Thisby
N. Plays Lion
O. What P & T talked through
P. Oberon sends Puck to find one struck by Cupid's arrow.
Q. Father of Hermia
R. A Midsummer Night's ___
S. Oberon commands Puck to anoint Demetrius's ___ as he sleeps.
T. Queen of the Amazons
U. Puck changes Bottom's head to that of an ___.
V. Wants to play all the roles
W. A ___ Night's Dream
X. Robin Goodfellow
Y. Tells Hermia's plans to Demetrius

Midsummer Night's Dream Matching 2 Answer Key

P - 1. FLOWER	A. Writes 'Pyramus and Thisby'
A - 2. QUINCE	B. 'Your eyes must look with his ___.'
R - 3. DREAM	C. Where plays are performed
S - 4. EYES	D. Arranges to meet Lysander in the woods
E - 5. WOODS	E. Where Lysander & Hermia agree to meet
C - 6. STAGE	F. Play division
X - 7. PUCK	G. Queen of the Fairies
F - 8. ACT	H. King of the Fairies
Q - 9. EGEUS	I. Hermia will have to live as one if she refuses to marry Demetrius.
G -10. TITANIA	J. Bottom wants one written for the play.
H -11. OBERON	K. Topic Theseus and Hippolyta discuss at play's start
K -12. WEDDING	L. Duke of Athens
T -13. HIPPOLYTA	M. Plays Thisby
D -14. HERMIA	N. Plays Lion
B -15. JUDGEMENT	O. What P & T talked through
Y -16. HELENA	P. Oberon sends Puck to find one struck by Cupid's arrow.
O -17. WALL	Q. Father of Hermia
U -18. ASS	R. A Midsummer Night's ___
N -19. SNUG	S. Oberon commands Puck to anoint Demetrius's ___ as he sleeps.
W -20. MIDSUMMER	T. Queen of the Amazons
M -21. FLUTE	U. Puck changes Bottom's head to that of an ___.
V -22. BOTTOM	V. Wants to play all the roles
I - 23. NUN	W. A ___ Night's Dream
J - 24. PROLOGUE	X. Robin Goodfellow
L - 25. THESEUS	Y. Tells Hermia's plans to Demetrius

Midsummer Night's Dream Matching 3

___ 1. OBERON
___ 2. JUDGEMENT
___ 3. HELENA
___ 4. HIPPOLYTA
___ 5. WEDDING
___ 6. SNUG
___ 7. SNOUT
___ 8. HERMIA
___ 9. PROLOGUE
___10. EYES
___11. DEMETRIUS
___12. STAGE
___13. MIDSUMMER
___14. DREAM
___15. ACT
___16. SCENE
___17. WALL
___18. LYSANDER
___19. FLUTE
___20. ASS
___21. THESEUS
___22. SHAKESPEARE
___23. TITANIA
___24. QUINCE
___25. BOTTOM

A. A ___ Night's Dream
B. Queen of the Amazons
C. Arranges to meet Lysander in the woods
D. Act division
E. Tells Hermia's plans to Demetrius
F. What P & T talked through
G. Plays Thisby
H. Author of MND
I. A Midsummer Night's ___
J. Queen of the Fairies
K. Play division
L. King of the Fairies
M. Oberon commands Puck to anoint Demetrius's ___ as he sleeps.
N. Topic Theseus and Hippolyta discuss at play's start
O. Wants to play all the roles
P. 'Your eyes must look with his ___.'
Q. Plays Wall
R. Writes 'Pyramus and Thisby'
S. Bottom wants one written for the play.
T. Plays Lion
U. Duke of Athens
V. Puck changes Bottom's head to that of an ___.
W. Hermia loves him.
X. Helena loves him, but he is to marry Hermia.
Y. Where plays are performed

Midsummer Night's Dream Matching 3 Answer Key

L - 1. OBERON	A. A ___ Night's Dream
P - 2. JUDGEMENT	B. Queen of the Amazons
E - 3. HELENA	C. Arranges to meet Lysander in the woods
B - 4. HIPPOLYTA	D. Act division
N - 5. WEDDING	E. Tells Hermia's plans to Demetrius
T - 6. SNUG	F. What P & T talked through
Q - 7. SNOUT	G. Plays Thisby
C - 8. HERMIA	H. Author of MND
S - 9. PROLOGUE	I. A Midsummer Night's ___
M - 10. EYES	J. Queen of the Fairies
X - 11. DEMETRIUS	K. Play division
Y - 12. STAGE	L. King of the Fairies
A - 13. MIDSUMMER	M. Oberon commands Puck to anoint Demetrius's ___ as he sleeps.
I - 14. DREAM	N. Topic Theseus and Hippolyta discuss at play's start
K - 15. ACT	O. Wants to play all the roles
D - 16. SCENE	P. 'Your eyes must look with his ___.'
F - 17. WALL	Q. Plays Wall
W - 18. LYSANDER	R. Writes 'Pyramus and Thisby'
G - 19. FLUTE	S. Bottom wants one written for the play.
V - 20. ASS	T. Plays Lion
U - 21. THESEUS	U. Duke of Athens
H - 22. SHAKESPEARE	V. Puck changes Bottom's head to that of an ___.
J - 23. TITANIA	W. Hermia loves him.
R - 24. QUINCE	X. Helena loves him, but he is to marry Hermia.
O - 25. BOTTOM	Y. Where plays are performed

Midsummer Night's Dream Matching 4

___ 1. WALL
___ 2. EYES
___ 3. JUDGEMENT
___ 4. EGEUS
___ 5. SHAKESPEARE
___ 6. NUN
___ 7. SNOUT
___ 8. DREAM
___ 9. WOODS
___ 10. HIPPOLYTA
___ 11. ACT
___ 12. QUINCE
___ 13. LOVE
___ 14. HELENA
___ 15. SCENE
___ 16. THESEUS
___ 17. FLUTE
___ 18. PROLOGUE
___ 19. MIDSUMMER
___ 20. OBERON
___ 21. WEDDING
___ 22. DEMETRIUS
___ 23. STAGE
___ 24. SNUG
___ 25. LYSANDER

A. Oberon commands Puck to anoint Demetrius's ___ as he sleeps.
B. A Midsummer Night's ___
C. Writes 'Pyramus and Thisby'
D. King of the Fairies
E. Tells Hermia's plans to Demetrius
F. Plays Thisby
G. Where plays are performed
H. Hermia loves him.
I. Queen of the Amazons
J. Hermia will have to live as one if she refuses to marry Demetrius.
K. 'Your eyes must look with his ___.'
L. Duke of Athens
M. What P & T talked through
N. Where Lysander & Hermia agree to meet
O. Plays Wall
P. Helena loves him, but he is to marry Hermia.
Q. Bottom wants one written for the play.
R. A ___ Night's Dream
S. Play division
T. Plays Lion
U. Act division
V. Topic Theseus and Hippolyta discuss at play's start
W. Author of MND
X. Father of Hermia
Y. Feeling Helena has for Demetrius

Midsummer Night's Dream Matching 4 Answer Key

M - 1. WALL	A.	Oberon commands Puck to anoint Demetrius's ___ as he sleeps.
A - 2. EYES	B.	A Midsummer Night's ___
K - 3. JUDGEMENT	C.	Writes 'Pyramus and Thisby'
X - 4. EGEUS	D.	King of the Fairies
W - 5. SHAKESPEARE	E.	Tells Hermia's plans to Demetrius
J - 6. NUN	F.	Plays Thisby
O - 7. SNOUT	G.	Where plays are performed
B - 8. DREAM	H.	Hermia loves him.
N - 9. WOODS	I.	Queen of the Amazons
I - 10. HIPPOLYTA	J.	Hermia will have to live as one if she refuses to marry Demetrius.
S - 11. ACT	K.	'Your eyes must look with his ___.'
C - 12. QUINCE	L.	Duke of Athens
Y - 13. LOVE	M.	What P & T talked through
E - 14. HELENA	N.	Where Lysander & Hermia agree to meet
U - 15. SCENE	O.	Plays Wall
L - 16. THESEUS	P.	Helena loves him, but he is to marry Hermia.
F - 17. FLUTE	Q.	Bottom wants one written for the play.
Q - 18. PROLOGUE	R.	A ___ Night's Dream
R - 19. MIDSUMMER	S.	Play division
D - 20. OBERON	T.	Plays Lion
V - 21. WEDDING	U.	Act division
P - 22. DEMETRIUS	V.	Topic Theseus and Hippolyta discuss at play's start
G - 23. STAGE	W.	Author of MND
T - 24. SNUG	X.	Father of Hermia
H - 25. LYSANDER	Y.	Feeling Helena has for Demetrius

Copyrighted

Midsummer Night's Dream Magic Squares 1

Match the definition with the vocabulary word. Put your answers in the magic squares below. When your answers are correct, all columns and rows will add to the same number.

A. LYSANDER
B. HERMIA
C. FLOWER
D. STAGE
E. FLUTE
F. HIPPOLYTA
G. WEDDING
H. SNUG
I. DEMETRIUS
J. WALL
K. PROLOGUE
L. DREAM
M. JUDGEMENT
N. TITANIA
O. SNOUT
P. SCENE

1. 'Your eyes must look with his ___.'
2. Queen of the Amazons
3. Plays Lion
4. Plays Wall
5. A Midsummer Night's ___
6. Oberon sends Puck to find one struck by Cupid's arrow.
7. Hermia loves him.
8. What P & T talked through
9. Bottom wants one written for the play.
10. Where plays are performed
11. Arranges to meet Lysander in the woods
12. Helena loves him, but he is to marry Hermia.
13. Queen of the Fairies
14. Plays Thisby
15. Topic Theseus and Hippolyta discuss at play's start
16. Act division

A=	B=	C=	D=
E=	F=	G=	H=
I=	J=	K=	L=
M=	N=	O=	P=

Midsummer Night's Dream Magic Squares 1 Answer Key

Match the definition with the vocabulary word. Put your answers in the magic squares below. When your answers are correct, all columns and rows will add to the same number.

A. LYSANDER
B. HERMIA
C. FLOWER
D. STAGE
E. FLUTE
F. HIPPOLYTA
G. WEDDING
H. SNUG
I. DEMETRIUS
J. WALL
K. PROLOGUE
L. DREAM
M. JUDGEMENT
N. TITANIA
O. SNOUT
P. SCENE

1. 'Your eyes must look with his ___.'
2. Queen of the Amazons
3. Plays Lion
4. Plays Wall
5. A Midsummer Night's ___
6. Oberon sends Puck to find one struck by Cupid's arrow.
7. Hermia loves him.
8. What P & T talked through
9. Bottom wants one written for the play.
10. Where plays are performed
11. Arranges to meet Lysander in the woods
12. Helena loves him, but he is to marry Hermia.
13. Queen of the Fairies
14. Plays Thisby
15. Topic Theseus and Hippolyta discuss at play's start
16. Act division

A=7	B=11	C=6	D=10
E=14	F=2	G=15	H=3
I=12	J=8	K=9	L=5
M=1	N=13	O=4	P=16

Midsummer Night's Dream Magic Squares 2

Match the definition with the vocabulary word. Put your answers in the magic squares below. When your answers are correct, all columns and rows will add to the same number.

A. ASS
B. HERMIA
C. EGEUS
D. FLUTE
E. PUCK
F. DEMETRIUS
G. FLOWER
H. ACT
I. BOTTOM
J. SHAKESPEARE
K. JUDGEMENT
L. DREAM
M. HIPPOLYTA
N. TITANIA
O. LOVE
P. MIDSUMMER

1. Father of Hermia
2. Author of MND
3. Helena loves him, but he is to marry Hermia.
4. Feeling Helena has for Demetrius
5. A ___ Night's Dream
6. Robin Goodfellow
7. Wants to play all the roles
8. Plays Thisby
9. Queen of the Amazons
10. Play division
11. A Midsummer Night's ___
12. Puck changes Bottom's head to that of an ___.
13. Arranges to meet Lysander in the woods
14. 'Your eyes must look with his ___.'
15. Oberon sends Puck to find one struck by Cupid's arrow.
16. Queen of the Fairies

A=	B=	C=	D=
E=	F=	G=	H=
I=	J=	K=	L=
M=	N=	O=	P=

23
Copyrighted

Midsummer Night's Dream Magic Squares 2 Answer Key

Match the definition with the vocabulary word. Put your answers in the magic squares below. When your answers are correct, all columns and rows will add to the same number.

A. ASS
B. HERMIA
C. EGEUS
D. FLUTE
E. PUCK
F. DEMETRIUS
G. FLOWER
H. ACT
I. BOTTOM
J. SHAKESPEARE
K. JUDGEMENT
L. DREAM
M. HIPPOLYTA
N. TITANIA
O. LOVE
P. MIDSUMMER

1. Father of Hermia
2. Author of MND
3. Helena loves him, but he is to marry Hermia.
4. Feeling Helena has for Demetrius
5. A ___ Night's Dream
6. Robin Goodfellow
7. Wants to play all the roles
8. Plays Thisby
9. Queen of the Amazons
10. Play division
11. A Midsummer Night's ___
12. Puck changes Bottom's head to that of an ___.
13. Arranges to meet Lysander in the woods
14. 'Your eyes must look with his ___.'
15. Oberon sends Puck to find one struck by Cupid's arrow.
16. Queen of the Fairies

A=12	B=13	C=1	D=8
E=6	F=3	G=15	H=10
I=7	J=2	K=14	L=11
M=9	N=16	O=4	P=5

Midsummer Night's Dream Magic Squares 3

Match the definition with the vocabulary word. Put your answers in the magic squares below. When your answers are correct, all columns and rows will add to the same number.

A. DEMETRIUS
B. BOTTOM
C. FLOWER
D. TITANIA
E. ASS
F. PROLOGUE
G. DREAM
H. LYSANDER
I. HIPPOLYTA
J. ACT
K. EGEUS
L. WALL
M. PUCK
N. HERMIA
O. STAGE
P. OBERON

1. Where plays are performed
2. Queen of the Fairies
3. Play division
4. Puck changes Bottom's head to that of an ___.
5. Queen of the Amazons
6. Bottom wants one written for the play.
7. King of the Fairies
8. Oberon sends Puck to find one struck by Cupid's arrow.
9. Hermia loves him.
10. Father of Hermia
11. Helena loves him, but he is to marry Hermia.
12. Arranges to meet Lysander in the woods
13. Wants to play all the roles
14. Robin Goodfellow
15. A Midsummer Night's ___
16. What P & T talked through

A=	B=	C=	D=
E=	F=	G=	H=
I=	J=	K=	L=
M=	N=	O=	P=

25
Copyrighted

Midsummer Night's Dream Magic Squares 3 Answer Key

Match the definition with the vocabulary word. Put your answers in the magic squares below. When your answers are correct, all columns and rows will add to the same number.

A. DEMETRIUS
B. BOTTOM
C. FLOWER
D. TITANIA
E. ASS
F. PROLOGUE
G. DREAM
H. LYSANDER
I. HIPPOLYTA
J. ACT
K. EGEUS
L. WALL
M. PUCK
N. HERMIA
O. STAGE
P. OBERON

1. Where plays are performed
2. Queen of the Fairies
3. Play division
4. Puck changes Bottom's head to that of an ___.
5. Queen of the Amazons
6. Bottom wants one written for the play.
7. King of the Fairies
8. Oberon sends Puck to find one struck by Cupid's arrow.
9. Hermia loves him.
10. Father of Hermia
11. Helena loves him, but he is to marry Hermia.
12. Arranges to meet Lysander in the woods
13. Wants to play all the roles
14. Robin Goodfellow
15. A Midsummer Night's ___
16. What P & T talked through

A=11	B=13	C=8	D=2
E=4	F=6	G=15	H=9
I=5	J=3	K=10	L=16
M=14	N=12	O=1	P=7

Midsummer Night's Dream Magic Squares 4

Match the definition with the vocabulary word. Put your answers in the magic squares below. When your answers are correct, all columns and rows will add to the same number.

A. PUCK
B. DEMETRIUS
C. OBERON
D. WOODS
E. PROLOGUE
F. QUINCE
G. EGEUS
H. LOVE
I. FLUTE
J. TITANIA
K. STAGE
L. DREAM
M. HERMIA
N. SCENE
O. FLOWER
P. HELENA

1. Robin Goodfellow
2. Act division
3. Queen of the Fairies
4. Bottom wants one written for the play.
5. Father of Hermia
6. A Midsummer Night's ___
7. Tells Hermia's plans to Demetrius
8. King of the Fairies
9. Oberon sends Puck to find one struck by Cupid's arrow.
10. Where Lysander & Hermia agree to meet
11. Feeling Helena has for Demetrius
12. Where plays are performed
13. Plays Thisby
14. Writes 'Pyramus and Thisby'
15. Helena loves him, but he is to marry Hermia.
16. Arranges to meet Lysander in the woods

A=	B=	C=	D=
E=	F=	G=	H=
I=	J=	K=	L=
M=	N=	O=	P=

27
Copyrighted

Midsummer Night's Dream Magic Squares 4 Answer Key

Match the definition with the vocabulary word. Put your answers in the magic squares below. When your answers are correct, all columns and rows will add to the same number.

A. PUCK
B. DEMETRIUS
C. OBERON
D. WOODS
E. PROLOGUE
F. QUINCE
G. EGEUS
H. LOVE
I. FLUTE
J. TITANIA
K. STAGE
L. DREAM
M. HERMIA
N. SCENE
O. FLOWER
P. HELENA

1. Robin Goodfellow
2. Act division
3. Queen of the Fairies
4. Bottom wants one written for the play.
5. Father of Hermia
6. A Midsummer Night's ___
7. Tells Hermia's plans to Demetrius
8. King of the Fairies
9. Oberon sends Puck to find one struck by Cupid's arrow.
10. Where Lysander & Hermia agree to meet
11. Feeling Helena has for Demetrius
12. Where plays are performed
13. Plays Thisby
14. Writes 'Pyramus and Thisby'
15. Helena loves him, but he is to marry Hermia.
16. Arranges to meet Lysander in the woods

A=1	B=15	C=8	D=10
E=4	F=14	G=5	H=11
I=13	J=3	K=12	L=6
M=16	N=2	O=9	P=7

Midsummer Night's Dream Word Search 1

Words are placed backwards, forward, diagonally, up and down. Clues listed below can help you find the words. Circle the hidden vocabulary words in the maze.

```
P U C K T J D W A S Q H E R M I A X S G
R W H Q Y U E T S N U G H Y P J V Q H F
O E I Y L D M P S O I W V D E Q W J A J
L D P Z L G E H J U N L K N R S F B K H
O D P W F E T T M T C G S F V Z B P E X
G I O W T M R X K S E D D W H Q H B S F
U N L Z H E I Q W N O P S G D J R P P C
E G Y J Q N U X R O H Q P C F P F X E Y
M P T M M T S Z W H L T D S F V S Q A W
J V A J D S D V L S X Q H N K J B M R T
Y M S W H S Y H J W S B N V Q W B V E L
N C X Z M X G Z X C S W H R B V P L K Q
G P K W G Q K B L R C M R F C N D W D F
D W Q G G V H J L Q N C C V V F N R B N
P B V M Q C Q B S F J Y X J K T Y N D R
V P T G W T H C S S D C Q Z L B M P P Q
D X G P N Q L S T H W G Z D P G I R K S
M D G Y D T K J J P T C S V G T D S S L
H C H A P M V Z L C T N K L J H S F G G
V P O I T Z M V P H R E S T C E U R F S
Z M B N Q O S W S E F K G S Q S M M F V
S L E A T W V X W L B R T E V E M A L L
N S R T A M A O X O T A H B U U E E U C
U U O I C X L L F V G E N E C S R R T Y
G B N T T F H E L E N A L Y S A N D E R
```

'Your eyes must look with his ___.' (9)
A Midsummer Night's ___ (5)
A ___ Night's Dream (9)
Act division (5)
Arranges to meet Lysander in the woods (6)
Author of MND (11)
Bottom wants one written for the play. (8)
Duke of Athens (7)
Father of Hermia (5)
Feeling Helena has for Demetrius (4)
Helena loves him, but he is to marry Hermia. (9)
Hermia loves him. (8)
Hermia will have to live as one if she refuses to marry Demetrius. (3)
King of the Fairies (6)
Oberon commands Puck to anoint Demetrius's ___ as he sleeps. (4)
Oberon sends Puck to find one struck by Cupid's arrow. (6)

Play division (3)
Plays Lion (4)
Plays Thisby (5)
Plays Wall (5)
Puck changes Bottom's head to that of an ___. (3)
Queen of the Amazons (9)
Queen of the Fairies (7)
Robin Goodfellow (4)
Tells Hermia's plans to Demetrius (6)
Topic Theseus and Hippolyta discuss at play's start (7)
Wants to play all the roles (6)
What P & T talked through (4)
Where Lysander & Hermia agree to meet (5)
Where plays are performed (5)
Writes 'Pyramus and Thisby' (6)

Midsummer Night's Dream Word Search 1 Answer Key

Words are placed backwards, forward, diagonally, up and down. Clues listed below can help you find the words. Circle the hidden vocabulary words in the maze.

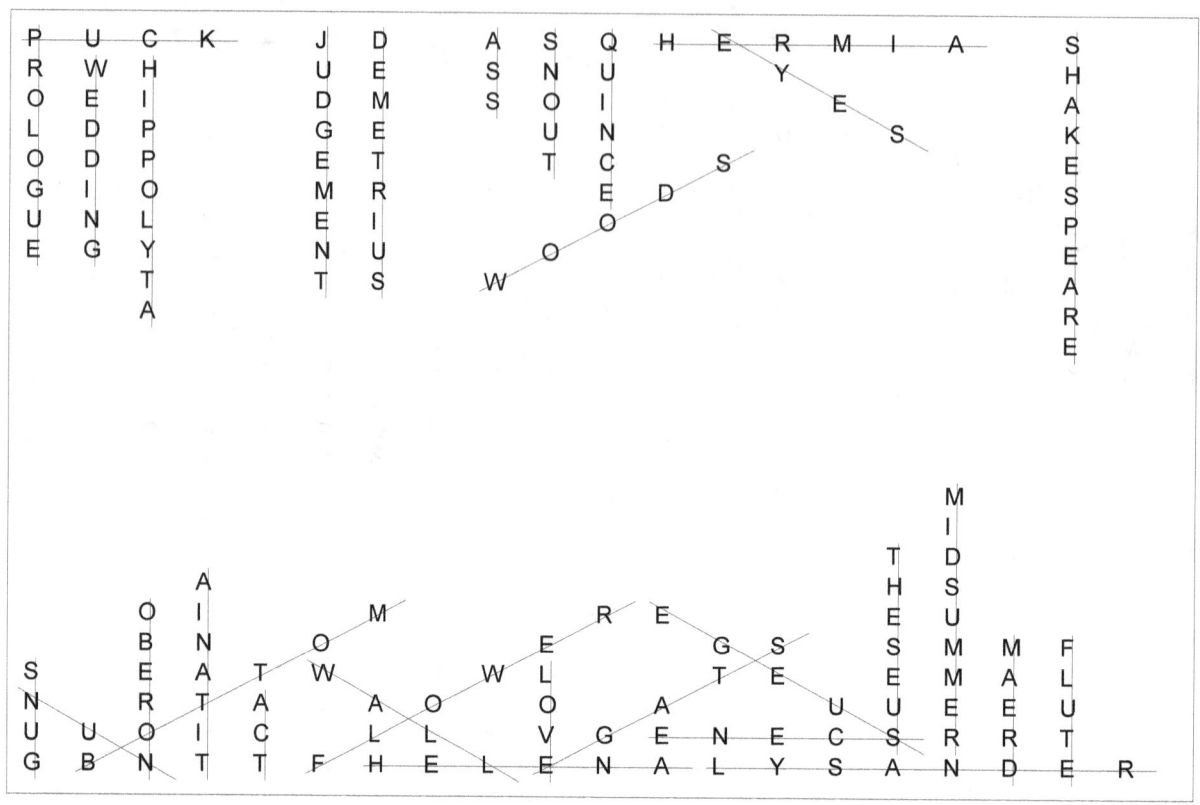

'Your eyes must look with his ___.' (9)
A Midsummer Night's ___ (5)
A ___ Night's Dream (9)
Act division (5)
Arranges to meet Lysander in the woods (6)
Author of MND (11)
Bottom wants one written for the play. (8)
Duke of Athens (7)
Father of Hermia (5)
Feeling Helena has for Demetrius (4)
Helena loves him, but he is to marry Hermia. (9)
Hermia loves him. (8)
Hermia will have to live as one if she refuses to marry Demetrius. (3)
King of the Fairies (6)
Oberon commands Puck to anoint Demetrius's ___ as he sleeps. (4)
Oberon sends Puck to find one struck by Cupid's arrow. (6)

Play division (3)
Plays Lion (4)
Plays Thisby (5)
Plays Wall (5)
Puck changes Bottom's head to that of an ___. (3)
Queen of the Amazons (9)
Queen of the Fairies (7)
Robin Goodfellow (4)
Tells Hermia's plans to Demetrius (6)
Topic Theseus and Hippolyta discuss at play's start (7)
Wants to play all the roles (6)
What P & T talked through (4)
Where Lysander & Hermia agree to meet (5)
Where plays are performed (5)
Writes 'Pyramus and Thisby' (6)

Midsummer Night's Dream Word Search 2

Words are placed backwards, forward, diagonally, up and down. Clues listed below can help you find the words. Circle the hidden vocabulary words in the maze.

```
C P R O L O G U E G T N Q C G P S S W L
M D W M L G K M T L Y T L D K H K H R R
J T W V N J K N R R K H L S V F W D D S
N D X M R X T R G Y S J G D K H J R Q S
V V V T V N G M R L L X K Y S W J X R G
L N Z C G D C G V Z Z K K H V C S D B B
X X V N Q J F P Y C K B K T Y W L F V R
H W M B V K S P H D P R H F W P B J Y S
L T S H L P J P R P L G Q H X X Y X L V
S G Q W K X K X D P N T Z N G K B Y L J
C R N D K D B B K V V N P F C H H K Y G
J Z Q A H K W Z J B H X R X Q H F V S X
D D T T F J M P J R N E G T V E P D A L
L J T Y T L B Z U H L T L K D R M X N S
R S Q L H B O R D G O Q A E V M S J D W
A Z S O E V C W G R V S S L N I N O E P
K C U P S U E G E N E C S E X A O U R R
B C T P E V J M M R F U C T I W U W N Z
O O B I U W M Y E G I N K N A Q T L J T
B Q T H S U F C N R I E A S F G L D Z H
E R N T S J K D T U B T X N L A E R Q K
R Q G D O M V E Q Q I U Q U W Y K E H Z
O B I V W M M R J T J L Y G Y N Y A M S
N M H L X E P N C P H F Y X T E F M L Y
G N I D D E W X R S H A K E S P E A R E
```

'Your eyes must look with his ___.' (9)
A Midsummer Night's ___ (5)
A ___ Night's Dream (9)
Act division (5)
Arranges to meet Lysander in the woods (6)
Author of MND (11)
Bottom wants one written for the play. (8)
Duke of Athens (7)
Father of Hermia (5)
Feeling Helena has for Demetrius (4)
Helena loves him, but he is to marry Hermia. (9)
Hermia loves him. (8)
Hermia will have to live as one if she refuses to marry Demetrius. (3)
King of the Fairies (6)
Oberon commands Puck to anoint Demetrius's ___ as he sleeps. (4)
Oberon sends Puck to find one struck by Cupid's arrow. (6)

Play division (3)
Plays Lion (4)
Plays Thisby (5)
Plays Wall (5)
Puck changes Bottom's head to that of an ___. (3)
Queen of the Amazons (9)
Queen of the Fairies (7)
Robin Goodfellow (4)
Tells Hermia's plans to Demetrius (6)
Topic Theseus and Hippolyta discuss at play's start (7)
Wants to play all the roles (6)
What P & T talked through (4)
Where Lysander & Hermia agree to meet (5)
Where plays are performed (5)
Writes 'Pyramus and Thisby' (6)

Midsummer Night's Dream Word Search 2 Answer Key

Words are placed backwards, forward, diagonally, up and down. Clues listed below can help you find the words. Circle the hidden vocabulary words in the maze.

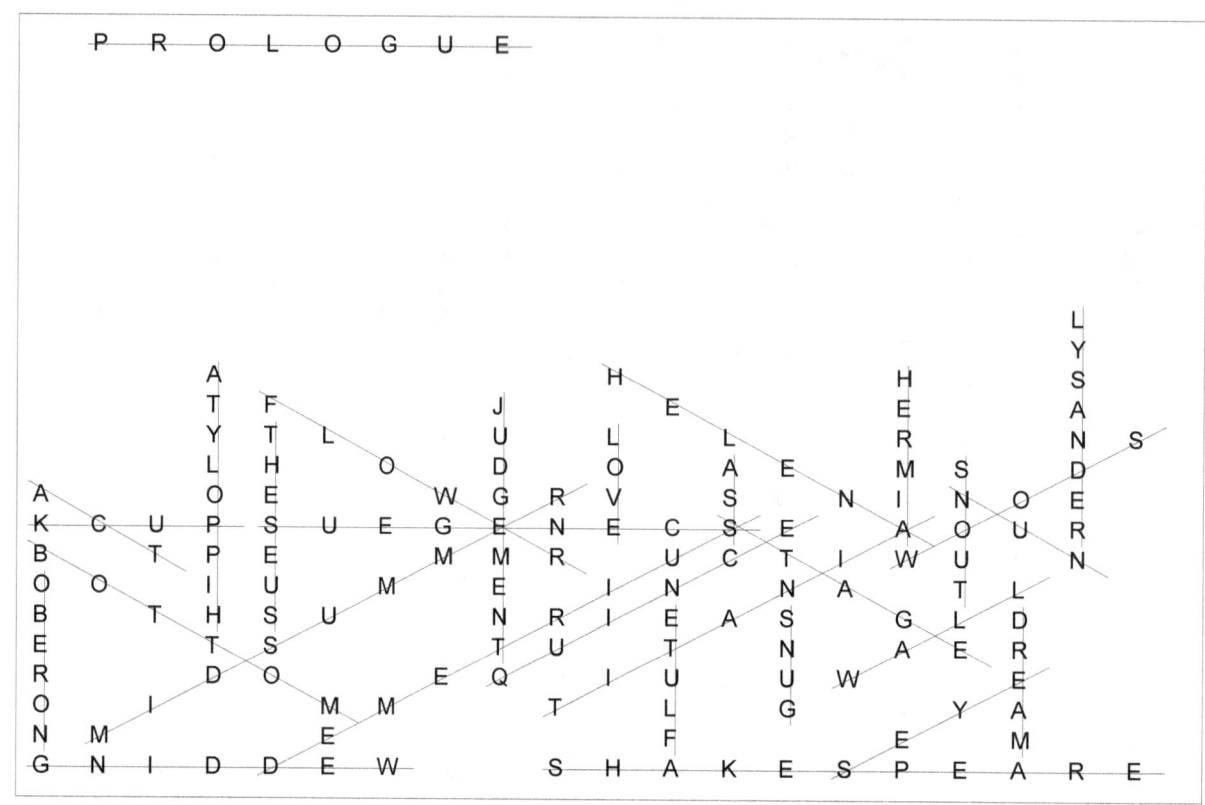

'Your eyes must look with his ___.' (9)
A Midsummer Night's ___ (5)
A ___ Night's Dream (9)
Act division (5)
Arranges to meet Lysander in the woods (6)
Author of MND (11)
Bottom wants one written for the play. (8)
Duke of Athens (7)
Father of Hermia (5)
Feeling Helena has for Demetrius (4)
Helena loves him, but he is to marry Hermia. (9)
Hermia loves him. (8)
Hermia will have to live as one if she refuses to marry Demetrius. (3)
King of the Fairies (6)
Oberon commands Puck to anoint Demetrius's ___ as he sleeps. (4)
Oberon sends Puck to find one struck by Cupid's arrow. (6)

Play division (3)
Plays Lion (4)
Plays Thisby (5)
Plays Wall (5)
Puck changes Bottom's head to that of an ___. (3)
Queen of the Amazons (9)
Queen of the Fairies (7)
Robin Goodfellow (4)
Tells Hermia's plans to Demetrius (6)
Topic Theseus and Hippolyta discuss at play's start (7)
Wants to play all the roles (6)
What P & T talked through (4)
Where Lysander & Hermia agree to meet (5)
Where plays are performed (5)
Writes 'Pyramus and Thisby' (6)

Midsummer Night's Dream Word Search 3

Words are placed backwards, forward, diagonally, up and down. Words listed below are included in the maze. Circle the hidden vocabulary words in the maze.

```
L W F B W O O D S E K W W H A T V Q H Z
O N L S O T Q J V Y F A E I R S F U E X
V P U D H T Q F L E L L D P Y V S I R M
E S T L E Z T E W S C L D P X S L N M P
P O E L N M U O Y R V C I O X G H C I J
Z B B N V G E T M R D X N L E Q C E A B
G K C E O N Z T F Q T L G Y M G H D T Q
Q G Z L R V B T R L R W L T V R E X D R
V Q O B E O T S X I O M W A C K L U N N
G R S T M V N X X T U W G S M W E F S T
P Y G P M H J F F D F S E L N B N N D V
M T S H U L Y L G V M X S R R T A R C C
B D K K S T F Y W B X B Z F G F S V S J
N D D Q D H X G Q H X V S M J M E L J L
V S K S I R P V C M T T Q U Q J R W Z B
D X W D M J H R F N D F D P C H A F X C
H R C T L M N C S N L G G G V J E G C N
E D T W Y K Q H B S E Z Q P X Y P N S B
G Z A F S L T N F M F B Z F U P S U D T
A C R S A S W U E F D T G K M C E Q R Y
T I T A N I A N S C E N E Y K S K X E S
S S Y O D U T V K V J C R D E N A P A T
K D U H E F G B R X H N H H P J H D M G
D T V J R D C W P M L V T G T M S V S M
X Q T Y H T B P V M M Q F R Z P D Z D L
```

ACT	FLUTE	NUN	SNUG
ASS	HELENA	OBERON	STAGE
BOTTOM	HERMIA	PROLOGUE	THESEUS
DEMETRIUS	HIPPOLYTA	PUCK	TITANIA
DREAM	JUDGEMENT	QUINCE	WALL
EGEUS	LOVE	SCENE	WEDDING
EYES	LYSANDER	SHAKESPEARE	WOODS
FLOWER	MIDSUMMER	SNOUT	

Midsummer Night's Dream Word Search 3 Answer Key

Words are placed backwards, forward, diagonally, up and down. Words listed below are included in the maze. Circle the hidden vocabulary words in the maze.

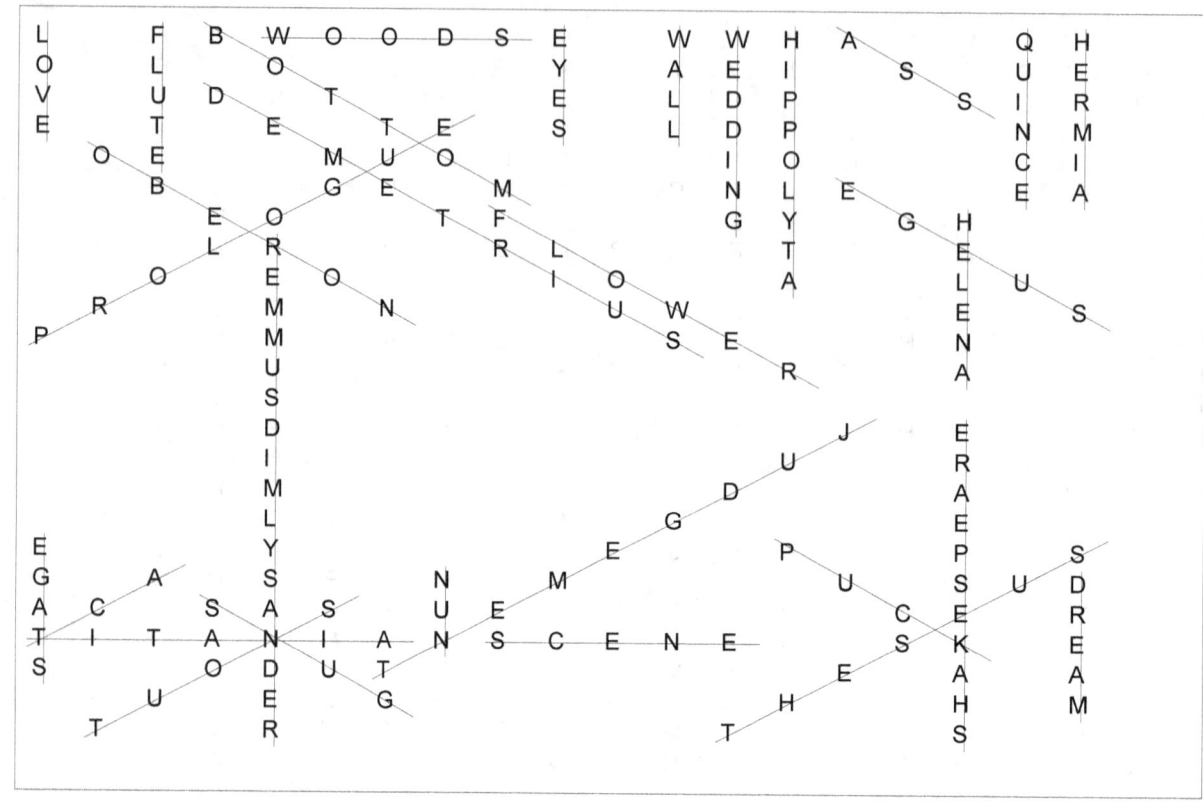

ACT	FLUTE	NUN	SNUG
ASS	HELENA	OBERON	STAGE
BOTTOM	HERMIA	PROLOGUE	THESEUS
DEMETRIUS	HIPPOLYTA	PUCK	TITANIA
DREAM	JUDGEMENT	QUINCE	WALL
EGEUS	LOVE	SCENE	WEDDING
EYES	LYSANDER	SHAKESPEARE	WOODS
FLOWER	MIDSUMMER	SNOUT	

Midsummer Night's Dream Word Search 4

Words are placed backwards, forward, diagonally, up and down. Words listed below are included in the maze. Circle the hidden vocabulary words in the maze.

```
F D R K W P N Q L Y B F R O J P G B H X
C W G D W R H X P Y X F K U B N M O E S
B G F J G Y I Q L K B Q D H K E M T Y S
C Q D N S F P D J D R G H D E F R T E N
S H A K E S P E A R E T S N U G Q O S C
P V F K G A O T Q M M F F H F N E M N G
R R L L W S L N E D M L W Q P N B U K C
W O O D S S Y N U S U E S E H T T L S T
N V W L Z N T C C N S N Q T H C L Y Y L
E P E K O Q A E V O D V N M A A X S Z H
Q U R X D G N N S U I X R J W G H A V H
U C W H R E U J Q T M V A N E P E N V W
I K W W E F L E H M N I D W D L R D C N
N H S N A L Z L M L N V L E D V M E K N
C Q E C M J S H K A C B T Z I F I R X W
E W C L D E M E T R I U S C N Z A J L R
M D H Q E P F I X K L J K Y G V G T V Z
Y T F T K N T W W F Q D F F Q D J H F V
P Z C R Q C A V F F H K R G P P C M T X
J H H B Z K M Q L F H F T F X J V G J S
K J X P H Q F N L W J Y S X G Z G S V C
J G H P C G S D R D H D B Q S R J P F T
T K P P S W M G T Z T C L C Z W D T N N
J D P F J G S S X B T W K F M R W B F Q
N K D F X M Q B T S X W G R D W M T T N
```

ACT	FLUTE	NUN	SNUG
ASS	HELENA	OBERON	STAGE
BOTTOM	HERMIA	PROLOGUE	THESEUS
DEMETRIUS	HIPPOLYTA	PUCK	TITANIA
DREAM	JUDGEMENT	QUINCE	WALL
EGEUS	LOVE	SCENE	WEDDING
EYES	LYSANDER	SHAKESPEARE	WOODS
FLOWER	MIDSUMMER	SNOUT	

Midsummer Night's Dream Word Search 4 Answer Key

Words are placed backwards, forward, diagonally, up and down. Words listed below are included in the maze. Circle the hidden vocabulary words in the maze.

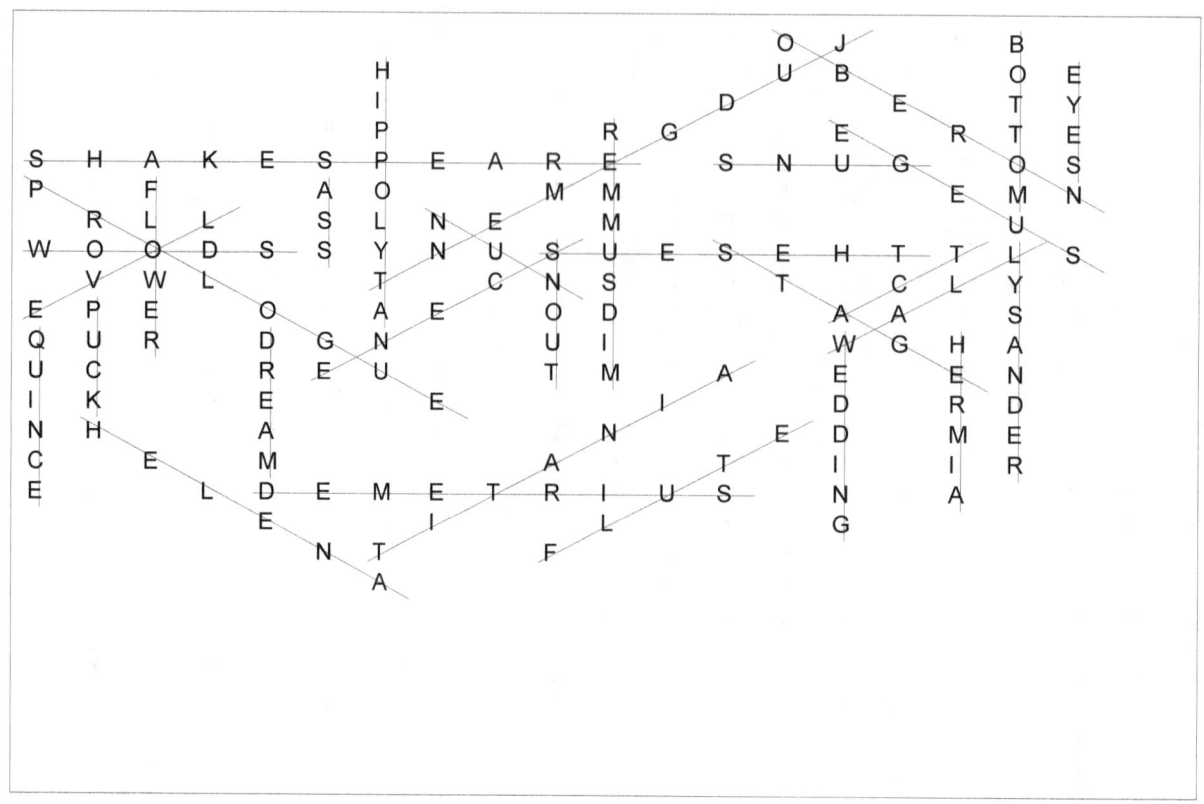

ACT	FLUTE	NUN	SNUG
ASS	HELENA	OBERON	STAGE
BOTTOM	HERMIA	PROLOGUE	THESEUS
DEMETRIUS	HIPPOLYTA	PUCK	TITANIA
DREAM	JUDGEMENT	QUINCE	WALL
EGEUS	LOVE	SCENE	WEDDING
EYES	LYSANDER	SHAKESPEARE	WOODS
FLOWER	MIDSUMMER	SNOUT	

Midsummer Night's Dream Crossword 1

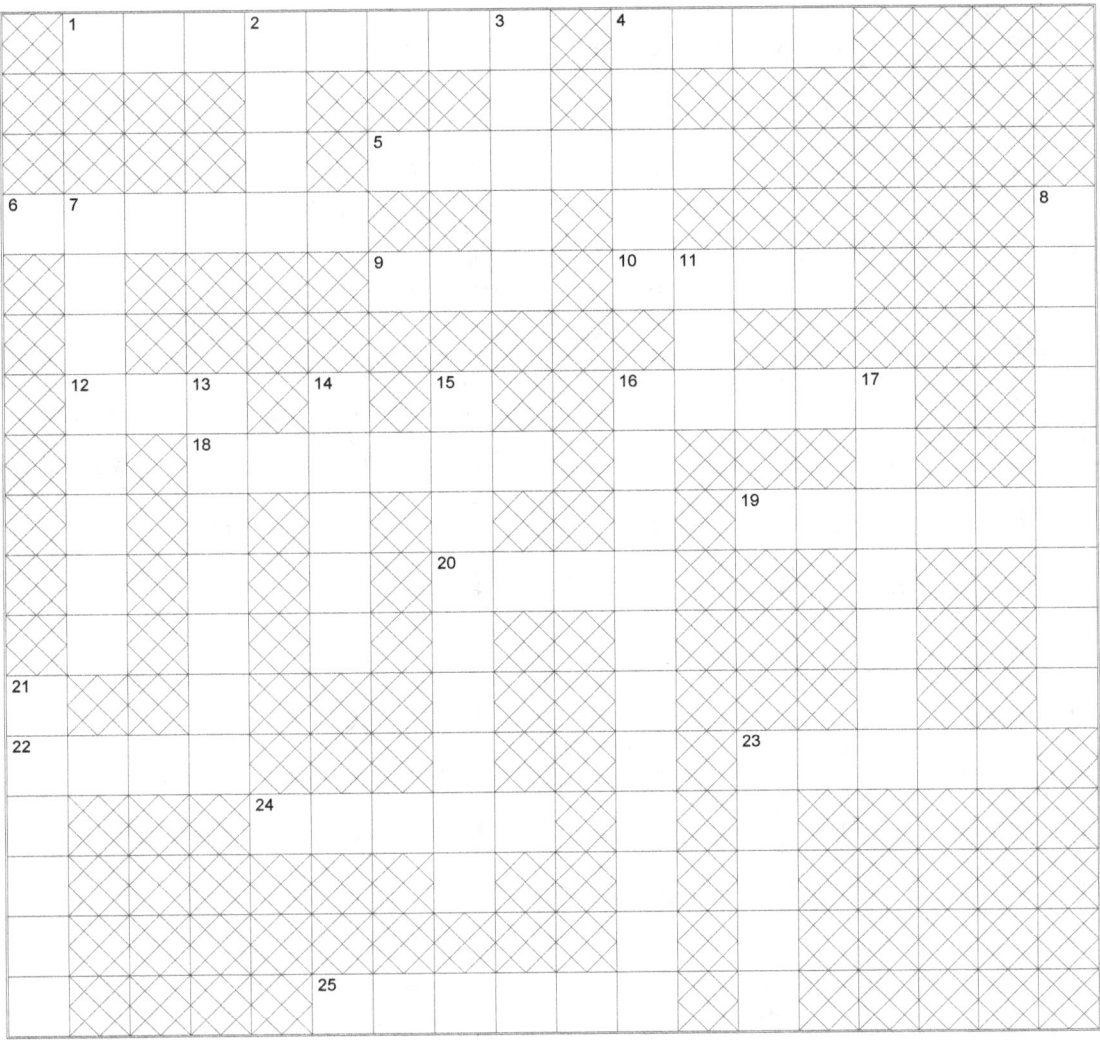

Across
1. Bottom wants one written for the play.
4. What P & T talked through
5. King of the Fairies
6. Oberon sends Puck to find one struck by Cupid's arrow.
9. Puck changes Bottom's head to that of an ___.
10. Plays Lion
12. Play division
16. Plays Wall
18. Arranges to meet Lysander in the woods
19. Wants to play all the roles
20. Robin Goodfellow
22. Oberon commands Puck to anoint Demetrius's ___ as he sleeps.
23. Where plays are performed
24. Plays Thisby
25. Writes 'Pyramus and Thisby'

Down
2. Feeling Helena has for Demetrius
3. Father of Hermia
4. Where Lysander & Hermia agree to meet
7. Hermia loves him.
8. 'Your eyes must look with his ___.'
11. Hermia will have to live as one if she refuses to marry Demetrius.
13. Duke of Athens
14. A Midsummer Night's ___
15. Queen of the Amazons
16. Author of MND
17. Queen of the Fairies
21. Tells Hermia's plans to Demetrius
23. Act division

Midsummer Night's Dream Crossword 1 Answer Key

	1 P	R	O	2 L	O	G	3 U	E		4 W	A	L	L		
				O			G			O					
				V		5 O	B	E	R	O	N				
6 F	7 L	O	W	E	R		U			D					8 J
	Y					9 A	S	S		10 S	11 N	U	G		U
	S										U				D
	12 A	C	13 T		14 D		15 H			16 S	N	O	17 U	T	G
	N		18 H	E	R	M	I	A		H			I		E
	D		E		E			P		A		19 B	O	T	T	O	M
	E		S		A		20 P	U	C	K			A		E
	R		E		M		O			E			N		N
21 H			U				L			S			I		T
22 E	Y	E	S				Y			P		23 S	T	A	G	E
L				24 F	L	U	T	E		E		C			
E							A			A		E			
N										R		N			
A				25 Q	U	I	N	C	E		E			

Across
1. Bottom wants one written for the play.
4. What P & T talked through
5. King of the Fairies
6. Oberon sends Puck to find one struck by Cupid's arrow.
9. Puck changes Bottom's head to that of an ___.
10. Plays Lion
12. Play division
16. Plays Wall
18. Arranges to meet Lysander in the woods
19. Wants to play all the roles
20. Robin Goodfellow
22. Oberon commands Puck to anoint Demetrius's ___ as he sleeps.
23. Where plays are performed
24. Plays Thisby
25. Writes 'Pyramus and Thisby'

Down
2. Feeling Helena has for Demetrius
3. Father of Hermia
4. Where Lysander & Hermia agree to meet
7. Hermia loves him.
8. 'Your eyes must look with his ___.'
11. Hermia will have to live as one if she refuses to marry Demetrius.
13. Duke of Athens
14. A Midsummer Night's ___
15. Queen of the Amazons
16. Author of MND
17. Queen of the Fairies
21. Tells Hermia's plans to Demetrius
23. Act division

Copyrighted

Midsummer Night's Dream Crossword 2

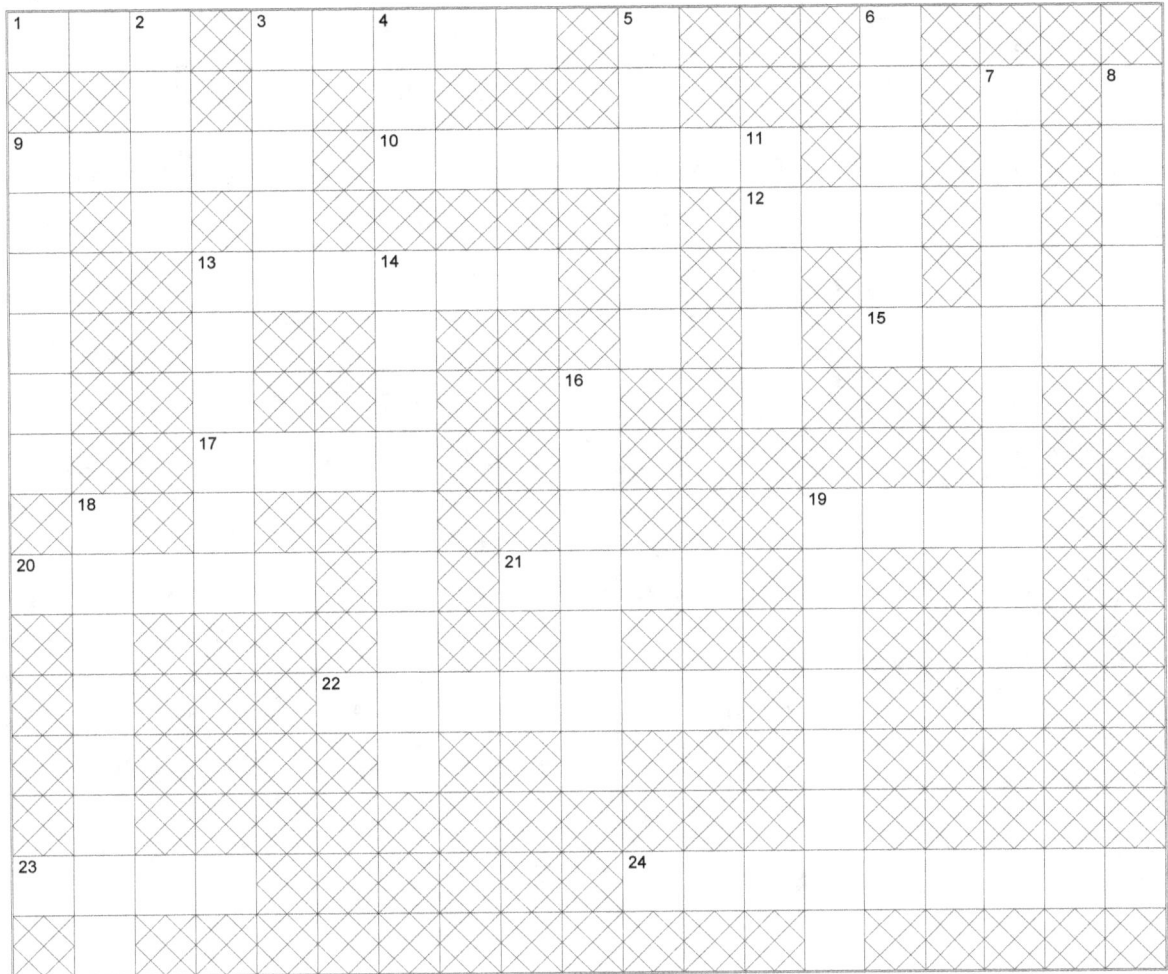

Across
1. Puck changes Bottom's head to that of an ___.
3. Where plays are performed
9. Plays Thisby
10. Duke of Athens
12. Hermia will have to live as one if she refuses to marry Demetrius.
13. Arranges to meet Lysander in the woods
15. Father of Hermia
17. Oberon commands Puck to anoint Demetrius's ___ as he sleeps.
19. Feeling Helena has for Demetrius
20. A Midsummer Night's ___
21. What P & T talked through
22. Topic Theseus and Hippolyta discuss at play's start
23. Robin Goodfellow
24. Helena loves him, but he is to marry Hermia.

Down
2. Plays Lion
3. Act division
4. Play division
5. King of the Fairies
6. Writes 'Pyramus and Thisby'
7. Author of MND
8. Where Lysander & Hermia agree to meet
9. Oberon sends Puck to find one struck by Cupid's arrow.
11. Plays Wall
13. Tells Hermia's plans to Demetrius
14. A ___ Night's Dream
16. Queen of the Fairies
18. Bottom wants one written for the play.
19. Hermia loves him.

Midsummer Night's Dream Crossword 2 Answer Key

	1 A	2 S	S		3 S	T	4 A	G	E		5 O			6 Q			
			N		C		C				B			U		7 S	8 W
9 F	L	U	T	E		10 T	H	E	S	E	U	S		11 I		H	O
L			G			N				R		12 N	U	N		A	O
O		13 H	E	R	14 M	I	A			O		C		K			D
W		E			I					N		U		15 E	G	E	U	S
E		L			D			16 T				T				S	
R		17 E	Y	E	S			I								P	
	18 P		N			U		T			19 L	O	V	E		
20 D	R	E	A	M		M		21 W	A	L	L		Y			A	
	O				M			N			S				R	
	L			22 W	E	D	D	I	N	G		A			E	
	O				R			A				N				
	G											D				
23 P	U	C	K					24 D	E	M	E	T	R	I	U	S
	E							R							

Across
1. Puck changes Bottom's head to that of an ___.
3. Where plays are performed
9. Plays Thisby
10. Duke of Athens
12. Hermia will have to live as one if she refuses to marry Demetrius.
13. Arranges to meet Lysander in the woods
15. Father of Hermia
17. Oberon commands Puck to anoint Demetrius's ___ as he sleeps.
19. Feeling Helena has for Demetrius
20. A Midsummer Night's ___
21. What P & T talked through
22. Topic Theseus and Hippolyta discuss at play's start
23. Robin Goodfellow
24. Helena loves him, but he is to marry Hermia.

Down
2. Plays Lion
3. Act division
4. Play division
5. King of the Fairies
6. Writes 'Pyramus and Thisby'
7. Author of MND
8. Where Lysander & Hermia agree to meet
9. Oberon sends Puck to find one struck by Cupid's arrow.
11. Plays Wall
13. Tells Hermia's plans to Demetrius
14. A ___ Night's Dream
16. Queen of the Fairies
18. Bottom wants one written for the play.
19. Hermia loves him.

Midsummer Night's Dream Crossword 3

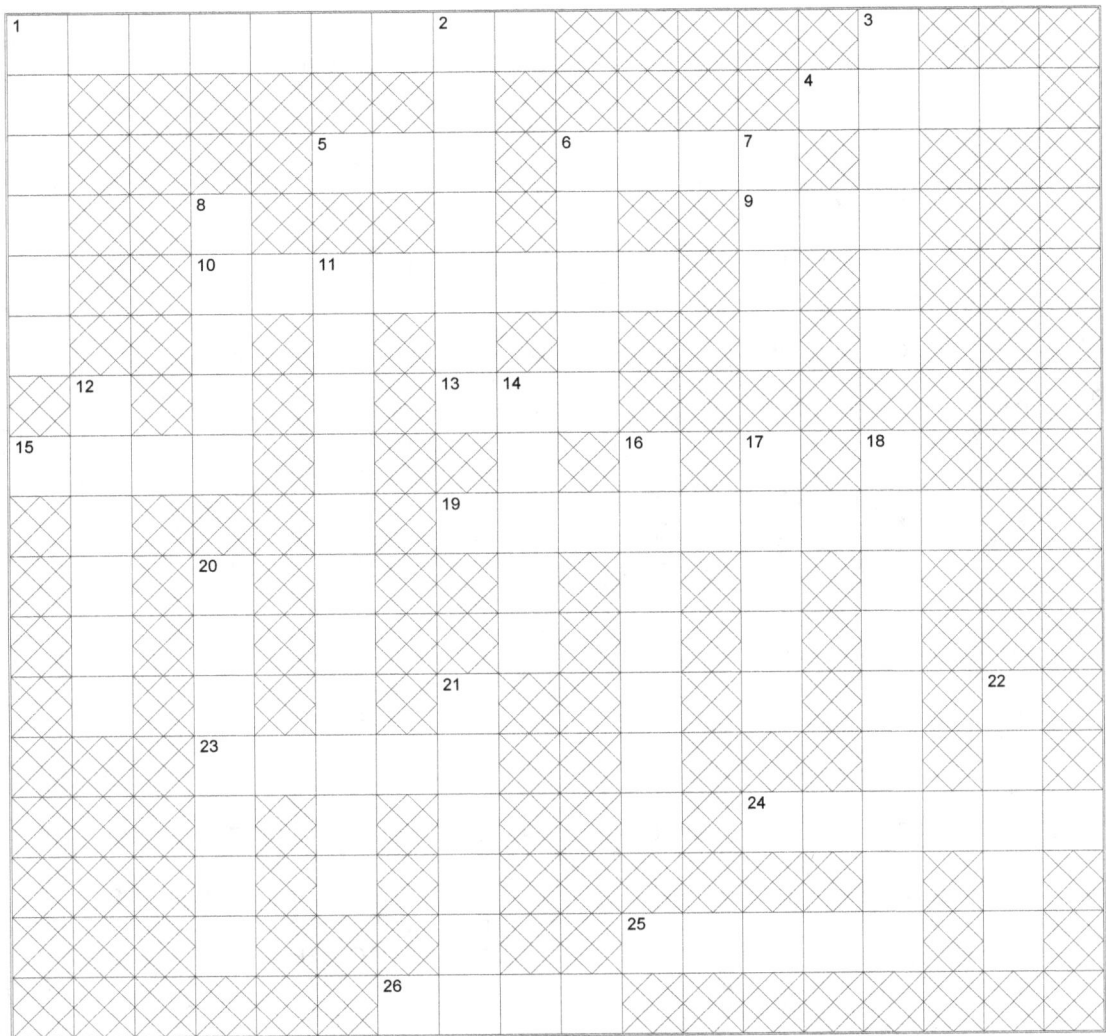

Across
1. Queen of the Amazons
4. Robin Goodfellow
5. Play division
6. Oberon commands Puck to anoint Demetrius's ___ as he sleeps.
9. Hermia will have to live as one if she refuses to marry Demetrius.
10. Hermia loves him.
13. Puck changes Bottom's head to that of an ___.
15. Feeling Helena has for Demetrius
19. Helena loves him, but he is to marry Hermia.
23. Where plays are performed
24. King of the Fairies
25. Plays Wall
26. What P & T talked through

Down
1. Tells Hermia's plans to Demetrius
2. Queen of the Fairies
3. Writes 'Pyramus and Thisby'
6. Father of Hermia
7. Plays Lion
8. Plays Thisby
11. Author of MND
12. Wants to play all the roles
14. Act division
16. Topic Theseus and Hippolyta discuss at play's start
17. A Midsummer Night's ___
18. 'Your eyes must look with his ___.'
20. Duke of Athens
21. Arranges to meet Lysander in the woods
22. Where Lysander & Hermia agree to meet

Midsummer Night's Dream Crossword 3 Answer Key

Across
1. Queen of the Amazons
4. Robin Goodfellow
5. Play division
6. Oberon commands Puck to anoint Demetrius's ___ as he sleeps.
9. Hermia will have to live as one if she refuses to marry Demetrius.
10. Hermia loves him.
13. Puck changes Bottom's head to that of an ___.
15. Feeling Helena has for Demetrius
19. Helena loves him, but he is to marry Hermia.
23. Where plays are performed
24. King of the Fairies
25. Plays Wall
26. What P & T talked through

Down
1. Tells Hermia's plans to Demetrius
2. Queen of the Fairies
3. Writes 'Pyramus and Thisby'
6. Father of Hermia
7. Plays Lion
8. Plays Thisby
11. Author of MND
12. Wants to play all the roles
14. Act division
16. Topic Theseus and Hippolyta discuss at play's start
17. A Midsummer Night's ___
18. 'Your eyes must look with his ___.'
20. Duke of Athens
21. Arranges to meet Lysander in the woods
22. Where Lysander & Hermia agree to meet

Midsummer Night's Dream Crossword 4

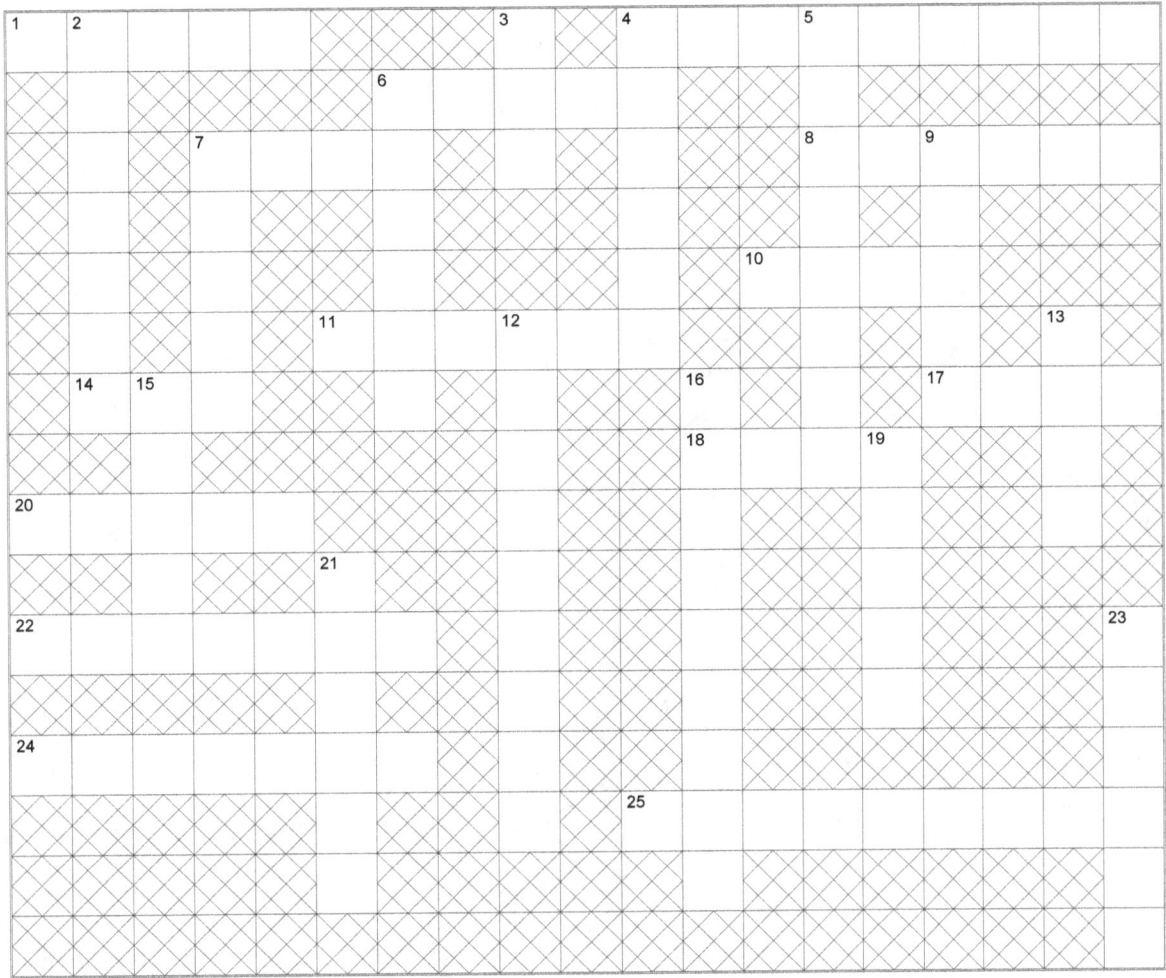

Across
1. Where plays are performed
4. Queen of the Amazons
6. Plays Thisby
7. What P & T talked through
8. King of the Fairies
10. Feeling Helena has for Demetrius
11. Arranges to meet Lysander in the woods
14. Puck changes Bottom's head to that of an ___.
17. Plays Lion
18. Oberon commands Puck to anoint Demetrius's ___ as he sleeps.
20. A Midsummer Night's ___
22. Duke of Athens
24. Topic Theseus and Hippolyta discuss at play's start
25. 'Your eyes must look with his ___.'

Down
2. Queen of the Fairies
3. Hermia will have to live as one if she refuses to marry Demetrius.
4. Tells Hermia's plans to Demetrius
5. Bottom wants one written for the play.
6. Oberon sends Puck to find one struck by Cupid's arrow.
7. Where Lysander & Hermia agree to meet
9. Father of Hermia
12. A ___ Night's Dream
13. Robin Goodfellow
15. Act division
16. Helena loves him, but he is to marry Hermia.
19. Plays Wall
21. Writes 'Pyramus and Thisby'
23. Wants to play all the roles

Midsummer Night's Dream Crossword 4 Answer Key

	1 S	2 T	A	G	E			3 N		4 H	I	P	5 P	O	L	Y	T	A
		I				6 F	L	U	T	E			R					
		T	7 W	A	L	L		N		L			8 O	B	9 E	R	O	N
		A		O		O				E			L		G			
		N		O		W				N		10 L	O	V	E			
		I		D		11 H	E	12 R	M	I	A		G		U		13 P	
	14 A	15 S	S			R		I			16 D		U		17 S	N	U	G
		C						D		18 E	Y	19 E	S				C	
20 D	R	E	A	M				S		M		N					K	
		N				21 Q		U		E		O						
22 T	H	E	S	E	U	S		M		T		U					23 B	
						I		M		R		T					O	
		24 W	E	D	D	I	N	G		I							T	
						C		E		25 J	U	D	G	E	M	E	N	T
						E		R		S							O	
																	M	

Across
1. Where plays are performed
4. Queen of the Amazons
6. Plays Thisby
7. What P & T talked through
8. King of the Fairies
10. Feeling Helena has for Demetrius
11. Arranges to meet Lysander in the woods
14. Puck changes Bottom's head to that of an ___.
17. Plays Lion
18. Oberon commands Puck to anoint Demetrius's ___ as he sleeps.
20. A Midsummer Night's ___
22. Duke of Athens
24. Topic Theseus and Hippolyta discuss at play's start
25. 'Your eyes must look with his ___.'

Down
2. Queen of the Fairies
3. Hermia will have to live as one if she refuses to marry Demetrius.
4. Tells Hermia's plans to Demetrius
5. Bottom wants one written for the play.
6. Oberon sends Puck to find one struck by Cupid's arrow.
7. Where Lysander & Hermia agree to meet
9. Father of Hermia
12. A ___ Night's Dream
13. Robin Goodfellow
15. Act division
16. Helena loves him, but he is to marry Hermia.
19. Plays Wall
21. Writes 'Pyramus and Thisby'
23. Wants to play all the roles

Midsummer Night's Dream

SNOUT	WEDDING	HERMIA	EYES	HIPPOLYTA
THESEUS	WOODS	NUN	LYSANDER	PUCK
TITANIA	STAGE	FREE SPACE	WALL	FLOWER
OBERON	MIDSUMMER	SCENE	HELENA	ASS
SHAKESPEARE	LOVE	DEMETRIUS	JUDGEMENT	ACT

Midsummer Night's Dream

PROLOGUE	SNUG	DREAM	FLUTE	EGEUS
BOTTOM	ACT	JUDGEMENT	DEMETRIUS	LOVE
SHAKESPEARE	ASS	FREE SPACE	SCENE	MIDSUMMER
OBERON	FLOWER	WALL	QUINCE	STAGE
TITANIA	PUCK	LYSANDER	NUN	WOODS

Midsummer Night's Dream

SHAKESPEARE	WOODS	DEMETRIUS	EGEUS	SCENE
OBERON	PUCK	SNOUT	WEDDING	TITANIA
HIPPOLYTA	THESEUS	FREE SPACE	ASS	MIDSUMMER
QUINCE	LOVE	FLOWER	WALL	HERMIA
ACT	DREAM	HELENA	BOTTOM	PROLOGUE

Midsummer Night's Dream

LYSANDER	FLUTE	EYES	NUN	JUDGEMENT
SNUG	PROLOGUE	BOTTOM	HELENA	DREAM
ACT	HERMIA	FREE SPACE	FLOWER	LOVE
QUINCE	MIDSUMMER	ASS	STAGE	THESEUS
HIPPOLYTA	TITANIA	WEDDING	SNOUT	PUCK

Midsummer Night's Dream

LOVE	PUCK	STAGE	EGEUS	PROLOGUE
SNUG	DREAM	THESEUS	NUN	SCENE
HIPPOLYTA	ACT	FREE SPACE	JUDGEMENT	SNOUT
DEMETRIUS	SHAKESPEARE	HELENA	QUINCE	TITANIA
WEDDING	FLUTE	LYSANDER	EYES	FLOWER

Midsummer Night's Dream

MIDSUMMER	OBERON	BOTTOM	HERMIA	WALL
ASS	FLOWER	EYES	LYSANDER	FLUTE
WEDDING	TITANIA	FREE SPACE	HELENA	SHAKESPEARE
DEMETRIUS	SNOUT	JUDGEMENT	WOODS	ACT
HIPPOLYTA	SCENE	NUN	THESEUS	DREAM

Midsummer Night's Dream

QUINCE	OBERON	DREAM	SHAKESPEARE	TITANIA
WOODS	HELENA	PROLOGUE	EYES	ASS
HIPPOLYTA	EGEUS	FREE SPACE	WALL	THESEUS
NUN	SNOUT	WEDDING	SNUG	PUCK
SCENE	JUDGEMENT	DEMETRIUS	FLOWER	MIDSUMMER

Midsummer Night's Dream

LOVE	LYSANDER	STAGE	FLUTE	ACT
HERMIA	MIDSUMMER	FLOWER	DEMETRIUS	JUDGEMENT
SCENE	PUCK	FREE SPACE	WEDDING	SNOUT
NUN	THESEUS	WALL	BOTTOM	EGEUS
HIPPOLYTA	ASS	EYES	PROLOGUE	HELENA

Midsummer Night's Dream

NUN	EYES	HELENA	JUDGEMENT	FLOWER
OBERON	ACT	MIDSUMMER	HERMIA	QUINCE
EGEUS	PUCK	FREE SPACE	BOTTOM	SCENE
STAGE	HIPPOLYTA	THESEUS	TITANIA	WEDDING
DREAM	FLUTE	ASS	LOVE	SNOUT

Midsummer Night's Dream

PROLOGUE	SHAKESPEARE	DEMETRIUS	WOODS	LYSANDER
WALL	SNOUT	LOVE	ASS	FLUTE
DREAM	WEDDING	FREE SPACE	THESEUS	HIPPOLYTA
STAGE	SCENE	BOTTOM	SNUG	PUCK
EGEUS	QUINCE	HERMIA	MIDSUMMER	ACT

Midsummer Night's Dream

STAGE	HELENA	LYSANDER	DREAM	PROLOGUE
SHAKESPEARE	TITANIA	DEMETRIUS	EYES	JUDGEMENT
THESEUS	ASS	FREE SPACE	MIDSUMMER	LOVE
FLUTE	FLOWER	EGEUS	HERMIA	SNOUT
PUCK	BOTTOM	QUINCE	ACT	HIPPOLYTA

Midsummer Night's Dream

SNUG	OBERON	WEDDING	SCENE	WOODS
WALL	HIPPOLYTA	ACT	QUINCE	BOTTOM
PUCK	SNOUT	FREE SPACE	EGEUS	FLOWER
FLUTE	LOVE	MIDSUMMER	NUN	ASS
THESEUS	JUDGEMENT	EYES	DEMETRIUS	TITANIA

50
Copyrighted

Midsummer Night's Dream

WALL	ACT	SCENE	QUINCE	FLOWER
LOVE	DEMETRIUS	OBERON	MIDSUMMER	DREAM
PUCK	TITANIA	FREE SPACE	HERMIA	JUDGEMENT
THESEUS	LYSANDER	EGEUS	SHAKESPEARE	STAGE
FLUTE	NUN	ASS	EYES	HIPPOLYTA

Midsummer Night's Dream

PROLOGUE	SNOUT	SNUG	WEDDING	WOODS
HELENA	HIPPOLYTA	EYES	ASS	NUN
FLUTE	STAGE	FREE SPACE	EGEUS	LYSANDER
THESEUS	JUDGEMENT	HERMIA	BOTTOM	TITANIA
PUCK	DREAM	MIDSUMMER	OBERON	DEMETRIUS

Midsummer Night's Dream

WEDDING	FLOWER	BOTTOM	DEMETRIUS	OBERON
HERMIA	DREAM	MIDSUMMER	QUINCE	STAGE
HELENA	NUN	FREE SPACE	LOVE	SHAKESPEARE
LYSANDER	WALL	PROLOGUE	SCENE	EYES
ACT	FLUTE	HIPPOLYTA	TITANIA	SNOUT

Midsummer Night's Dream

THESEUS	EGEUS	ASS	WOODS	JUDGEMENT
SNUG	SNOUT	TITANIA	HIPPOLYTA	FLUTE
ACT	EYES	FREE SPACE	PROLOGUE	WALL
LYSANDER	SHAKESPEARE	LOVE	PUCK	NUN
HELENA	STAGE	QUINCE	MIDSUMMER	DREAM

Midsummer Night's Dream

HIPPOLYTA	THESEUS	NUN	SHAKESPEARE	JUDGEMENT
WOODS	LYSANDER	WALL	BOTTOM	SNUG
STAGE	HELENA	FREE SPACE	OBERON	WEDDING
EYES	LOVE	FLUTE	ASS	SCENE
EGEUS	DEMETRIUS	PROLOGUE	PUCK	HERMIA

Midsummer Night's Dream

DREAM	TITANIA	ACT	MIDSUMMER	FLOWER
SNOUT	HERMIA	PUCK	PROLOGUE	DEMETRIUS
EGEUS	SCENE	FREE SPACE	FLUTE	LOVE
EYES	WEDDING	OBERON	QUINCE	HELENA
STAGE	SNUG	BOTTOM	WALL	LYSANDER

Midsummer Night's Dream

QUINCE	HERMIA	DREAM	WALL	BOTTOM
OBERON	THESEUS	EGEUS	WEDDING	JUDGEMENT
FLOWER	LYSANDER	FREE SPACE	HELENA	PUCK
TITANIA	STAGE	LOVE	WOODS	FLUTE
SNUG	EYES	ACT	SCENE	MIDSUMMER

Midsummer Night's Dream

SNOUT	ASS	SHAKESPEARE	DEMETRIUS	NUN
PROLOGUE	MIDSUMMER	SCENE	ACT	EYES
SNUG	FLUTE	FREE SPACE	LOVE	STAGE
TITANIA	PUCK	HELENA	HIPPOLYTA	LYSANDER
FLOWER	JUDGEMENT	WEDDING	EGEUS	THESEUS

Midsummer Night's Dream

HELENA	THESEUS	EGEUS	JUDGEMENT	BOTTOM
MIDSUMMER	WOODS	PROLOGUE	STAGE	SCENE
EYES	ACT	FREE SPACE	WALL	FLUTE
OBERON	PUCK	WEDDING	LYSANDER	SNOUT
LOVE	DEMETRIUS	HIPPOLYTA	SNUG	QUINCE

Midsummer Night's Dream

ASS	DREAM	HERMIA	FLOWER	NUN
TITANIA	QUINCE	SNUG	HIPPOLYTA	DEMETRIUS
LOVE	SNOUT	FREE SPACE	WEDDING	PUCK
OBERON	FLUTE	WALL	SHAKESPEARE	ACT
EYES	SCENE	STAGE	PROLOGUE	WOODS

Midsummer Night's Dream

STAGE	WOODS	DEMETRIUS	ACT	WALL
THESEUS	SCENE	MIDSUMMER	HELENA	SHAKESPEARE
FLOWER	ASS	FREE SPACE	PUCK	EYES
DREAM	EGEUS	TITANIA	SNOUT	FLUTE
HIPPOLYTA	LYSANDER	OBERON	HERMIA	BOTTOM

Midsummer Night's Dream

WEDDING	PROLOGUE	SNUG	QUINCE	LOVE
JUDGEMENT	BOTTOM	HERMIA	OBERON	LYSANDER
HIPPOLYTA	FLUTE	FREE SPACE	TITANIA	EGEUS
DREAM	EYES	PUCK	NUN	ASS
FLOWER	SHAKESPEARE	HELENA	MIDSUMMER	SCENE

Midsummer Night's Dream

LYSANDER	PROLOGUE	PUCK	ASS	EYES
DEMETRIUS	SHAKESPEARE	MIDSUMMER	FLOWER	THESEUS
WEDDING	HELENA	FREE SPACE	ACT	FLUTE
WALL	STAGE	HIPPOLYTA	DREAM	HERMIA
SNOUT	SCENE	EGEUS	BOTTOM	QUINCE

Midsummer Night's Dream

JUDGEMENT	SNUG	TITANIA	NUN	WOODS
LOVE	QUINCE	BOTTOM	EGEUS	SCENE
SNOUT	HERMIA	FREE SPACE	HIPPOLYTA	STAGE
WALL	FLUTE	ACT	OBERON	HELENA
WEDDING	THESEUS	FLOWER	MIDSUMMER	SHAKESPEARE

Midsummer Night's Dream

HELENA	NUN	SNOUT	HIPPOLYTA	FLOWER
MIDSUMMER	THESEUS	SCENE	BOTTOM	WOODS
SHAKESPEARE	FLUTE	FREE SPACE	QUINCE	HERMIA
OBERON	DEMETRIUS	TITANIA	ASS	LYSANDER
EGEUS	WEDDING	DREAM	ACT	PROLOGUE

Midsummer Night's Dream

PUCK	LOVE	EYES	STAGE	SNUG
JUDGEMENT	PROLOGUE	ACT	DREAM	WEDDING
EGEUS	LYSANDER	FREE SPACE	TITANIA	DEMETRIUS
OBERON	HERMIA	QUINCE	WALL	FLUTE
SHAKESPEARE	WOODS	BOTTOM	SCENE	THESEUS

Midsummer Night's Dream

WEDDING	EYES	PROLOGUE	TITANIA	OBERON
WALL	JUDGEMENT	WOODS	DEMETRIUS	HIPPOLYTA
LOVE	MIDSUMMER	FREE SPACE	FLOWER	ASS
FLUTE	SNUG	STAGE	HERMIA	PUCK
QUINCE	BOTTOM	SHAKESPEARE	LYSANDER	THESEUS

Midsummer Night's Dream

ACT	NUN	HELENA	DREAM	EGEUS
SCENE	THESEUS	LYSANDER	SHAKESPEARE	BOTTOM
QUINCE	PUCK	FREE SPACE	STAGE	SNUG
FLUTE	ASS	FLOWER	SNOUT	MIDSUMMER
LOVE	HIPPOLYTA	DEMETRIUS	WOODS	JUDGEMENT

Midsummer Night's Dream

SNUG	WEDDING	WOODS	STAGE	QUINCE
OBERON	SCENE	SNOUT	ACT	THESEUS
WALL	MIDSUMMER	FREE SPACE	LOVE	HELENA
HERMIA	DEMETRIUS	BOTTOM	PUCK	PROLOGUE
DREAM	JUDGEMENT	TITANIA	FLOWER	FLUTE

Midsummer Night's Dream

SHAKESPEARE	NUN	EGEUS	EYES	ASS
HIPPOLYTA	FLUTE	FLOWER	TITANIA	JUDGEMENT
DREAM	PROLOGUE	FREE SPACE	BOTTOM	DEMETRIUS
HERMIA	HELENA	LOVE	LYSANDER	MIDSUMMER
WALL	THESEUS	ACT	SNOUT	SCENE

Midsummer Night's Dream Vocabulary Word List

No.	Word	Clue/Definition
1.	ABJURE	Give up; abstain from
2.	AMIABLE	Friendly and agreeable; good-natured
3.	AMOROUS	Strongly attracted or disposed to love
4.	AUDACIOUS	Bold, insolent, spirited, or original
5.	BASE	The lowest or bottom part
6.	BEGUILED	Deluded; cheated; diverted
7.	BOWER	Woman's private chamber in a medieval castle
8.	BRAKE	A thicket; small woods
9.	BROACHED	Pierced in order to draw off liquid
10.	CHAPLET	Wreath or garland for the head
11.	CHINK	Narrow opening; a crack
12.	CLAMOROUS	Noisy
13.	CONJUNCTION	Joint or simultaneous occurrence; done together
14.	CONSECRATED	Sacred
15.	DISCOURSE	Verbal expression in speech or writing
16.	DISCRETION	Ability or power to decide responsibly
17.	DOTAGE	Deterioration of mental faculties; senility
18.	DULCET	Pleasing to the ear; melodious
19.	ENAMORED	Inspired with love; captivated
20.	ENMITY	Deep-seated, often mutual, hatred
21.	ENTWIST	Twist together
22.	EXTEMPORE	Spoken or carried out with little preparation
23.	FILCHED	Snitched; stole
24.	FLOUT	Show contempt for
25.	FRET	Worry
26.	KINDRED	Relating to family
27.	KNAVERY	Unprincipled, crafty acts
28.	LAMENTABLE	Worthy of grief, mourning, or regret
29.	LOATH	Unwilling or reluctant
30.	MIRTH	Gladness; gaiety
31.	PERFORCE	By necessity; by force of circumstances
32.	PERJURED	Testified falsely under oath; falsified; untrue
33.	PERSUASION	Strongly held opinion; conviction
34.	PROMONTORY	High ridge of land jutting out into water
35.	PURGE	Remove (impurities) by or as if by cleansing
36.	REBUKE	Criticize or reprimand
37.	RECOUNT	Narrate the facts or details of
38.	REVENUE	Income; wealth; money
39.	RHEUMATIC	Suffering from aches in the muscles, joints, or bones
40.	SHROUD	Cloth used to wrap a body for burial
41.	SPRITE	Ghost or soul
42.	SPURN	Kick at or tread on disdainfully
43.	TARRYING	Remaining temporarily
44.	UNDISTINGUISHABLE	Having no unique markings; can't be clearly seen
45.	UPBRAID	To reproach
46.	VALOR	Bravery; courage
47.	VISAGE	Face; appearance

Midsummer Night's Dream Vocabulary Fill In The Blanks 1

_____ 1. Strongly held opinion; conviction

_____ 2. Having no unique markings; can't be clearly seen

_____ 3. Verbal expression in speech or writing

_____ 4. Worry

_____ 5. Unprincipled, crafty acts

_____ 6. Show contempt for

_____ 7. Snitched; stole

_____ 8. Deep-seated, often mutual, hatred

_____ 9. Spoken or carried out with little preparation

_____ 10. Suffering from aches in the muscles, joints, or bones

_____ 11. Cloth used to wrap a body for burial

_____ 12. Kick at or tread on disdainfully

_____ 13. Criticize or reprimand

_____ 14. Pleasing to the ear; melodious

_____ 15. Inspired with love; captivated

_____ 16. Joint or simultaneous occurrence; done together

_____ 17. Narrow opening; a crack

_____ 18. Remove (impurities) by or as if by cleansing

_____ 19. Worthy of grief, mourning, or regret

_____ 20. Sacred

Midsummer Night's Dream Vocabulary Fill In The Blanks 1 Answer Key

PERSUASION	1. Strongly held opinion; conviction
UNDISTINGUISHABLE	2. Having no unique markings; can't be clearly seen
DISCOURSE	3. Verbal expression in speech or writing
FRET	4. Worry
KNAVERY	5. Unprincipled, crafty acts
FLOUT	6. Show contempt for
FILCHED	7. Snitched; stole
ENMITY	8. Deep-seated, often mutual, hatred
EXTEMPORE	9. Spoken or carried out with little preparation
RHEUMATIC	10. Suffering from aches in the muscles, joints, or bones
SHROUD	11. Cloth used to wrap a body for burial
SPURN	12. Kick at or tread on disdainfully
REBUKE	13. Criticize or reprimand
DULCET	14. Pleasing to the ear; melodious
ENAMORED	15. Inspired with love; captivated
CONJUNCTION	16. Joint or simultaneous occurrence; done together
CHINK	17. Narrow opening; a crack
PURGE	18. Remove (impurities) by or as if by cleansing
LAMENTABLE	19. Worthy of grief, mourning, or regret
CONSECRATED	20. Sacred

Midsummer Night's Dream Vocabulary Fill In The Blanks 2

_____ 1. Narrate the facts or details of
_____ 2. Give up; abstain from
_____ 3. Narrow opening; a crack
_____ 4. Kick at or tread on disdainfully
_____ 5. Inspired with love; captivated
_____ 6. A thicket; small woods
_____ 7. Deluded; cheated; diverted
_____ 8. Deep-seated, often mutual, hatred
_____ 9. High ridge of land jutting out into water
_____ 10. Ghost or soul
_____ 11. Remove (impurities) by or as if by cleansing
_____ 12. Woman's private chamber in a medieval castle
_____ 13. Strongly attracted or disposed to love
_____ 14. Cloth used to wrap a body for burial
_____ 15. Worthy of grief, mourning, or regret
_____ 16. Face; appearance
_____ 17. Suffering from aches in the muscles, joints, or bones
_____ 18. Relating to family
_____ 19. Testified falsely under oath; falsified; untrue
_____ 20. Gladness; gaiety

Midsummer Night's Dream Vocabulary Fill In The Blanks 2 Answer Key

RECOUNT	1. Narrate the facts or details of
ABJURE	2. Give up; abstain from
CHINK	3. Narrow opening; a crack
SPURN	4. Kick at or tread on disdainfully
ENAMORED	5. Inspired with love; captivated
BRAKE	6. A thicket; small woods
BEGUILED	7. Deluded; cheated; diverted
ENMITY	8. Deep-seated, often mutual, hatred
PROMONTORY	9. High ridge of land jutting out into water
SPRITE	10. Ghost or soul
PURGE	11. Remove (impurities) by or as if by cleansing
BOWER	12. Woman's private chamber in a medieval castle
AMOROUS	13. Strongly attracted or disposed to love
SHROUD	14. Cloth used to wrap a body for burial
LAMENTABLE	15. Worthy of grief, mourning, or regret
VISAGE	16. Face; appearance
RHEUMATIC	17. Suffering from aches in the muscles, joints, or bones
KINDRED	18. Relating to family
PERJURED	19. Testified falsely under oath; falsified; untrue
MIRTH	20. Gladness; gaiety

Midsummer Night's Dream Vocabulary Fill In The Blanks 3

_____ 1. Friendly and agreeable; good-natured

_____ 2. To reproach

_____ 3. Pierced in order to draw off liquid

_____ 4. Bold, insolent, spirited, or original

_____ 5. Worry

_____ 6. Deterioration of mental faculties; senility

_____ 7. Give up; abstain from

_____ 8. Wreath or garland for the head

_____ 9. Remaining temporarily

_____ 10. Worthy of grief, mourning, or regret

_____ 11. Pleasing to the ear; melodious

_____ 12. Having no unique markings; can't be clearly seen

_____ 13. Ability or power to decide responsibly

_____ 14. The lowest or bottom part

_____ 15. Suffering from aches in the muscles, joints, or bones

_____ 16. Bravery; courage

_____ 17. Remove (impurities) by or as if by cleansing

_____ 18. Income; wealth; money

_____ 19. Inspired with love; captivated

_____ 20. By necessity; by force of circumstances

Midsummer Night's Dream Vocabulary Fill In The Blanks 3 Answer Key

AMIABLE	1. Friendly and agreeable; good-natured
UPBRAID	2. To reproach
BROACHED	3. Pierced in order to draw off liquid
AUDACIOUS	4. Bold, insolent, spirited, or original
FRET	5. Worry
DOTAGE	6. Deterioration of mental faculties; senility
ABJURE	7. Give up; abstain from
CHAPLET	8. Wreath or garland for the head
TARRYING	9. Remaining temporarily
LAMENTABLE	10. Worthy of grief, mourning, or regret
DULCET	11. Pleasing to the ear; melodious
UNDISTINGUISHABLE	12. Having no unique markings; can't be clearly seen
DISCRETION	13. Ability or power to decide responsibly
BASE	14. The lowest or bottom part
RHEUMATIC	15. Suffering from aches in the muscles, joints, or bones
VALOR	16. Bravery; courage
PURGE	17. Remove (impurities) by or as if by cleansing
REVENUE	18. Income; wealth; money
ENAMORED	19. Inspired with love; captivated
PERFORCE	20. By necessity; by force of circumstances

Midsummer Night's Dream Vocabulary Fill In The Blanks 4

_____ 1. Relating to family

_____ 2. Snitched; stole

_____ 3. Gladness; gaiety

_____ 4. Suffering from aches in the muscles, joints, or bones

_____ 5. Criticize or reprimand

_____ 6. Inspired with love; captivated

_____ 7. Spoken or carried out with little preparation

_____ 8. Show contempt for

_____ 9. Deterioration of mental faculties; senility

_____ 10. Friendly and agreeable; good-natured

_____ 11. Woman's private chamber in a medieval castle

_____ 12. By necessity; by force of circumstances

_____ 13. Noisy

_____ 14. Worry

_____ 15. To reproach

_____ 16. Ability or power to decide responsibly

_____ 17. Unprincipled, crafty acts

_____ 18. Twist together

_____ 19. Kick at or tread on disdainfully

_____ 20. Wreath or garland for the head

Midsummer Night's Dream Vocabulary Fill In The Blanks 4 Answer Key

KINDRED	1. Relating to family
FILCHED	2. Snitched; stole
MIRTH	3. Gladness; gaiety
RHEUMATIC	4. Suffering from aches in the muscles, joints, or bones
REBUKE	5. Criticize or reprimand
ENAMORED	6. Inspired with love; captivated
EXTEMPORE	7. Spoken or carried out with little preparation
FLOUT	8. Show contempt for
DOTAGE	9. Deterioration of mental faculties; senility
AMIABLE	10. Friendly and agreeable; good-natured
BOWER	11. Woman's private chamber in a medieval castle
PERFORCE	12. By necessity; by force of circumstances
CLAMOROUS	13. Noisy
FRET	14. Worry
UPBRAID	15. To reproach
DISCRETION	16. Ability or power to decide responsibly
KNAVERY	17. Unprincipled, crafty acts
ENTWIST	18. Twist together
SPURN	19. Kick at or tread on disdainfully
CHAPLET	20. Wreath or garland for the head

Midsummer Night's Dream Vocabulary Matching 1

___ 1. BEGUILED   A. Friendly and agreeable; good-natured
___ 2. CONJUNCTION   B. A thicket; small woods
___ 3. MIRTH   C. Gladness; gaiety
___ 4. PERFORCE   D. To reproach
___ 5. REVENUE   E. Narrow opening; a crack
___ 6. PERJURED   F. Wreath or garland for the head
___ 7. BOWER   G. Narrate the facts or details of
___ 8. TARRYING   H. The lowest or bottom part
___ 9. FLOUT   I. Worthy of grief, mourning, or regret
___10. AUDACIOUS   J. Show contempt for
___11. PROMONTORY   K. Suffering from aches in the muscles, joints, or bones
___12. RHEUMATIC   L. Bravery; courage
___13. VALOR   M. Snitched; stole
___14. CHINK   N. Unwilling or reluctant
___15. AMIABLE   O. Remaining temporarily
___16. BRAKE   P. Income; wealth; money
___17. BASE   Q. Testified falsely under oath; falsified; untrue
___18. LOATH   R. Deluded; cheated; diverted
___19. FILCHED   S. High ridge of land jutting out into water
___20. CHAPLET   T. Joint or simultaneous occurrence; done together
___21. KNAVERY   U. Unprincipled, crafty acts
___22. RECOUNT   V. Bold, insolent, spirited, or original
___23. UPBRAID   W. Woman's private chamber in a medieval castle
___24. ENTWIST   X. Twist together
___25. LAMENTABLE   Y. By necessity; by force of circumstances

Midsummer Night's Dream Vocabulary Matching 1 Answer Key

R - 1. BEGUILED	A.	Friendly and agreeable; good-natured
T - 2. CONJUNCTION	B.	A thicket; small woods
C - 3. MIRTH	C.	Gladness; gaiety
Y - 4. PERFORCE	D.	To reproach
P - 5. REVENUE	E.	Narrow opening; a crack
Q - 6. PERJURED	F.	Wreath or garland for the head
W - 7. BOWER	G.	Narrate the facts or details of
O - 8. TARRYING	H.	The lowest or bottom part
J - 9. FLOUT	I.	Worthy of grief, mourning, or regret
V - 10. AUDACIOUS	J.	Show contempt for
S - 11. PROMONTORY	K.	Suffering from aches in the muscles, joints, or bones
K - 12. RHEUMATIC	L.	Bravery; courage
L - 13. VALOR	M.	Snitched; stole
E - 14. CHINK	N.	Unwilling or reluctant
A - 15. AMIABLE	O.	Remaining temporarily
B - 16. BRAKE	P.	Income; wealth; money
H - 17. BASE	Q.	Testified falsely under oath; falsified; untrue
N - 18. LOATH	R.	Deluded; cheated; diverted
M - 19. FILCHED	S.	High ridge of land jutting out into water
F - 20. CHAPLET	T.	Joint or simultaneous occurrence; done together
U - 21. KNAVERY	U.	Unprincipled, crafty acts
G - 22. RECOUNT	V.	Bold, insolent, spirited, or original
D - 23. UPBRAID	W.	Woman's private chamber in a medieval castle
X - 24. ENTWIST	X.	Twist together
I - 25. LAMENTABLE	Y.	By necessity; by force of circumstances

Midsummer Night's Dream Vocabulary Matching 2

___ 1. ENMITY   A. Unprincipled, crafty acts
___ 2. FLOUT   B. Criticize or reprimand
___ 3. RECOUNT   C. Cloth used to wrap a body for burial
___ 4. ABJURE   D. Ghost or soul
___ 5. AMOROUS   E. Strongly attracted or disposed to love
___ 6. CONJUNCTION   F. Unwilling or reluctant
___ 7. KNAVERY   G. Deep-seated, often mutual, hatred
___ 8. PURGE   H. The lowest or bottom part
___ 9. PERJURED   I. Narrow opening; a crack
___10. LOATH   J. To reproach
___11. SHROUD   K. Joint or simultaneous occurrence; done together
___12. CLAMOROUS   L. Noisy
___13. BROACHED   M. Woman's private chamber in a medieval castle
___14. BOWER   N. By necessity; by force of circumstances
___15. CHINK   O. Kick at or tread on disdainfully
___16. BRAKE   P. Show contempt for
___17. UPBRAID   Q. Deluded; cheated; diverted
___18. BEGUILED   R. Give up; abstain from
___19. BASE   S. Having no unique markings; can't be clearly seen
___20. SPRITE   T. Testified falsely under oath; falsified; untrue
___21. PERFORCE   U. Remove (impurities) by or as if by cleansing
___22. UNDISTINGUISHABLE V. A thicket; small woods
___23. SPURN   W. Narrate the facts or details of
___24. REBUKE   X. Spoken or carried out with little preparation
___25. EXTEMPORE   Y. Pierced in order to draw off liquid

Midsummer Night's Dream Vocabulary Matching 2 Answer Key

G - 1. ENMITY	A.	Unprincipled, crafty acts
P - 2. FLOUT	B.	Criticize or reprimand
W - 3. RECOUNT	C.	Cloth used to wrap a body for burial
R - 4. ABJURE	D.	Ghost or soul
E - 5. AMOROUS	E.	Strongly attracted or disposed to love
K - 6. CONJUNCTION	F.	Unwilling or reluctant
A - 7. KNAVERY	G.	Deep-seated, often mutual, hatred
U - 8. PURGE	H.	The lowest or bottom part
T - 9. PERJURED	I.	Narrow opening; a crack
F - 10. LOATH	J.	To reproach
C - 11. SHROUD	K.	Joint or simultaneous occurrence; done together
L - 12. CLAMOROUS	L.	Noisy
Y - 13. BROACHED	M.	Woman's private chamber in a medieval castle
M - 14. BOWER	N.	By necessity; by force of circumstances
I - 15. CHINK	O.	Kick at or tread on disdainfully
V - 16. BRAKE	P.	Show contempt for
J - 17. UPBRAID	Q.	Deluded; cheated; diverted
Q - 18. BEGUILED	R.	Give up; abstain from
H - 19. BASE	S.	Having no unique markings; can't be clearly seen
D - 20. SPRITE	T.	Testified falsely under oath; falsified; untrue
N - 21. PERFORCE	U.	Remove (impurities) by or as if by cleansing
S - 22. UNDISTINGUISHABLE	V.	A thicket; small woods
O - 23. SPURN	W.	Narrate the facts or details of
B - 24. REBUKE	X.	Spoken or carried out with little preparation
X - 25. EXTEMPORE	Y.	Pierced in order to draw off liquid

Midsummer Night's Dream Vocabulary Matching 3

___ 1. LOATH
___ 2. CONJUNCTION
___ 3. KNAVERY
___ 4. PROMONTORY
___ 5. DOTAGE
___ 6. VISAGE
___ 7. REVENUE
___ 8. ENMITY
___ 9. BROACHED
___10. TARRYING
___11. PERSUASION
___12. PERFORCE
___13. BOWER
___14. KINDRED
___15. CHINK
___16. REBUKE
___17. RECOUNT
___18. CHAPLET
___19. VALOR
___20. SPRITE
___21. SHROUD
___22. FRET
___23. DISCOURSE
___24. CONSECRATED
___25. AMOROUS

A. Ghost or soul
B. Remaining temporarily
C. Strongly attracted or disposed to love
D. Deep-seated, often mutual, hatred
E. Worry
F. Relating to family
G. Narrate the facts or details of
H. High ridge of land jutting out into water
I. Deterioration of mental faculties; senility
J. Income; wealth; money
K. Strongly held opinion; conviction
L. Unwilling or reluctant
M. Face; appearance
N. Pierced in order to draw off liquid
O. Criticize or reprimand
P. Narrow opening; a crack
Q. Unprincipled, crafty acts
R. Bravery; courage
S. Joint or simultaneous occurrence; done together
T. Verbal expression in speech or writing
U. Sacred
V. By necessity; by force of circumstances
W. Woman's private chamber in a medieval castle
X. Wreath or garland for the head
Y. Cloth used to wrap a body for burial

Midsummer Night's Dream Vocabulary Matching 3 Answer Key

L - 1.	LOATH	A.	Ghost or soul
S - 2.	CONJUNCTION	B.	Remaining temporarily
Q - 3.	KNAVERY	C.	Strongly attracted or disposed to love
H - 4.	PROMONTORY	D.	Deep-seated, often mutual, hatred
I - 5.	DOTAGE	E.	Worry
M - 6.	VISAGE	F.	Relating to family
J - 7.	REVENUE	G.	Narrate the facts or details of
D - 8.	ENMITY	H.	High ridge of land jutting out into water
N - 9.	BROACHED	I.	Deterioration of mental faculties; senility
B - 10.	TARRYING	J.	Income; wealth; money
K - 11.	PERSUASION	K.	Strongly held opinion; conviction
V - 12.	PERFORCE	L.	Unwilling or reluctant
W - 13.	BOWER	M.	Face; appearance
F - 14.	KINDRED	N.	Pierced in order to draw off liquid
P - 15.	CHINK	O.	Criticize or reprimand
O - 16.	REBUKE	P.	Narrow opening; a crack
G - 17.	RECOUNT	Q.	Unprincipled, crafty acts
X - 18.	CHAPLET	R.	Bravery; courage
R - 19.	VALOR	S.	Joint or simultaneous occurrence; done together
A - 20.	SPRITE	T.	Verbal expression in speech or writing
Y - 21.	SHROUD	U.	Sacred
E - 22.	FRET	V.	By necessity; by force of circumstances
T - 23.	DISCOURSE	W.	Woman's private chamber in a medieval castle
U - 24.	CONSECRATED	X.	Wreath or garland for the head
C - 25.	AMOROUS	Y.	Cloth used to wrap a body for burial

Midsummer Night's Dream Vocabulary Matching 4

___ 1. TARRYING	A. Unwilling or reluctant
___ 2. RECOUNT	B. Worthy of grief, mourning, or regret
___ 3. PERJURED	C. A thicket; small woods
___ 4. UPBRAID	D. Testified falsely under oath; falsified; untrue
___ 5. KINDRED	E. Deep-seated, often mutual, hatred
___ 6. FILCHED	F. Having no unique markings; can't be clearly seen
___ 7. BROACHED	G. Relating to family
___ 8. DISCRETION	H. Pleasing to the ear; melodious
___ 9. AMIABLE	I. Cloth used to wrap a body for burial
___ 10. UNDISTINGUISHABLE	J. Give up; abstain from
___ 11. DULCET	K. Narrow opening; a crack
___ 12. BOWER	L. Strongly held opinion; conviction
___ 13. DOTAGE	M. Friendly and agreeable; good-natured
___ 14. AUDACIOUS	N. Sacred
___ 15. KNAVERY	O. Narrate the facts or details of
___ 16. ABJURE	P. Pierced in order to draw off liquid
___ 17. LAMENTABLE	Q. Snitched; stole
___ 18. LOATH	R. Deterioration of mental faculties; senility
___ 19. SHROUD	S. Remaining temporarily
___ 20. CONSECRATED	T. Strongly attracted or disposed to love
___ 21. CHINK	U. Unprincipled, crafty acts
___ 22. PERSUASION	V. Woman's private chamber in a medieval castle
___ 23. BRAKE	W. Bold, insolent, spirited, or original
___ 24. ENMITY	X. Ability or power to decide responsibly
___ 25. AMOROUS	Y. To reproach

Midsummer Night's Dream Vocabulary Matching 4 Answer Key

- S - 1. TARRYING
- O - 2. RECOUNT
- D - 3. PERJURED
- Y - 4. UPBRAID
- G - 5. KINDRED
- Q - 6. FILCHED
- P - 7. BROACHED
- X - 8. DISCRETION
- M - 9. AMIABLE
- F - 10. UNDISTINGUISHABLE
- H - 11. DULCET
- V - 12. BOWER
- R - 13. DOTAGE
- W - 14. AUDACIOUS
- U - 15. KNAVERY
- J - 16. ABJURE
- B - 17. LAMENTABLE
- A - 18. LOATH
- I - 19. SHROUD
- N - 20. CONSECRATED
- K - 21. CHINK
- L - 22. PERSUASION
- C - 23. BRAKE
- E - 24. ENMITY
- T - 25. AMOROUS

A. Unwilling or reluctant
B. Worthy of grief, mourning, or regret
C. A thicket; small woods
D. Testified falsely under oath; falsified; untrue
E. Deep-seated, often mutual, hatred
F. Having no unique markings; can't be clearly seen
G. Relating to family
H. Pleasing to the ear; melodious
I. Cloth used to wrap a body for burial
J. Give up; abstain from
K. Narrow opening; a crack
L. Strongly held opinion; conviction
M. Friendly and agreeable; good-natured
N. Sacred
O. Narrate the facts or details of
P. Pierced in order to draw off liquid
Q. Snitched; stole
R. Deterioration of mental faculties; senility
S. Remaining temporarily
T. Strongly attracted or disposed to love
U. Unprincipled, crafty acts
V. Woman's private chamber in a medieval castle
W. Bold, insolent, spirited, or original
X. Ability or power to decide responsibly
Y. To reproach

Midsummer Night's Dream Vocabulary Magic Squares 1

Match the definition with the vocabulary word. Put your answers in the magic squares below. When your answers are correct, all columns and rows will add to the same number.

A. UNDISTINGUISHABLE
B. BRAKE
C. DOTAGE
D. ENTWIST
E. RECOUNT
F. AUDACIOUS
G. CHAPLET
H. SHROUD
I. SPURN
J. KINDRED
K. BASE
L. DISCRETION
M. PERJURED
N. BEGUILED
O. DISCOURSE
P. MIRTH

1. Cloth used to wrap a body for burial
2. Having no unique markings; can't be clearly seen
3. A thicket; small woods
4. Wreath or garland for the head
5. Relating to family
6. Verbal expression in speech or writing
7. Gladness; gaiety
8. Kick at or tread on disdainfully
9. The lowest or bottom part
10. Deluded; cheated; diverted
11. Testified falsely under oath; falsified; untrue
12. Ability or power to decide responsibly
13. Narrate the facts or details of
14. Twist together
15. Deterioration of mental faculties; senility
16. Bold, insolent, spirited, or original

A=	B=	C=	D=
E=	F=	G=	H=
I=	J=	K=	L=
M=	N=	O=	P=

Midsummer Night's Dream Vocabulary Magic Squares 1 Answer Key

Match the definition with the vocabulary word. Put your answers in the magic squares below. When your answers are correct, all columns and rows will add to the same number.

A. UNDISTINGUISHABLE
B. BRAKE
C. DOTAGE
D. ENTWIST
E. RECOUNT
F. AUDACIOUS
G. CHAPLET
H. SHROUD
I. SPURN
J. KINDRED
K. BASE
L. DISCRETION
M. PERJURED
N. BEGUILED
O. DISCOURSE
P. MIRTH

1. Cloth used to wrap a body for burial
2. Having no unique markings; can't be clearly seen
3. A thicket; small woods
4. Wreath or garland for the head
5. Relating to family
6. Verbal expression in speech or writing
7. Gladness; gaiety
8. Kick at or tread on disdainfully
9. The lowest or bottom part
10. Deluded; cheated; diverted
11. Testified falsely under oath; falsified; untrue
12. Ability or power to decide responsibly
13. Narrate the facts or details of
14. Twist together
15. Deterioration of mental faculties; senility
16. Bold, insolent, spirited, or original

A=2	B=3	C=15	D=14
E=13	F=16	G=4	H=1
I=8	J=5	K=9	L=12
M=11	N=10	O=6	P=7

Midsummer Night's Dream Vocabulary Magic Squares 2

Match the definition with the vocabulary word. Put your answers in the magic squares below. When your answers are correct, all columns and rows will add to the same number.

A. LAMENTABLE
B. KNAVERY
C. SPURN
D. AMOROUS
E. EXTEMPORE
F. BASE
G. SHROUD
H. CONSECRATED
I. ENAMORED
J. CONJUNCTION
K. KINDRED
L. SPRITE
M. LOATH
N. DISCRETION
O. UPBRAID
P. CLAMOROUS

1. Kick at or tread on disdainfully
2. Joint or simultaneous occurrence; done together
3. The lowest or bottom part
4. To reproach
5. Noisy
6. Spoken or carried out with little preparation
7. Inspired with love; captivated
8. Strongly attracted or disposed to love
9. Unwilling or reluctant
10. Sacred
11. Ghost or soul
12. Worthy of grief, mourning, or regret
13. Unprincipled, crafty acts
14. Relating to family
15. Cloth used to wrap a body for burial
16. Ability or power to decide responsibly

A=	B=	C=	D=
E=	F=	G=	H=
I=	J=	K=	L=
M=	N=	O=	P=

Midsummer Night's Dream Vocabulary Magic Squares 2 Answer Key

Match the definition with the vocabulary word. Put your answers in the magic squares below. When your answers are correct, all columns and rows will add to the same number.

A. LAMENTABLE
B. KNAVERY
C. SPURN
D. AMOROUS
E. EXTEMPORE
F. BASE
G. SHROUD
H. CONSECRATED
I. ENAMORED
J. CONJUNCTION
K. KINDRED
L. SPRITE
M. LOATH
N. DISCRETION
O. UPBRAID
P. CLAMOROUS

1. Kick at or tread on disdainfully
2. Joint or simultaneous occurrence; done together
3. The lowest or bottom part
4. To reproach
5. Noisy
6. Spoken or carried out with little preparation
7. Inspired with love; captivated
8. Strongly attracted or disposed to love
9. Unwilling or reluctant
10. Sacred
11. Ghost or soul
12. Worthy of grief, mourning, or regret
13. Unprincipled, crafty acts
14. Relating to family
15. Cloth used to wrap a body for burial
16. Ability or power to decide responsibly

A=12	B=13	C=1	D=8
E=6	F=3	G=15	H=10
I=7	J=2	K=14	L=11
M=9	N=16	O=4	P=5

Midsummer Night's Dream Vocabulary Magic Squares 3

Match the definition with the vocabulary word. Put your answers in the magic squares below. When your answers are correct, all columns and rows will add to the same number.

A. SHROUD
B. SPRITE
C. UNDISTINGUISHABLE
D. DISCOURSE
E. CLAMOROUS
F. UPBRAID
G. RHEUMATIC
H. KNAVERY
I. CHAPLET
J. ENTWIST
K. DISCRETION
L. EXTEMPORE
M. MIRTH
N. BRAKE
O. DOTAGE
P. FLOUT

1. Cloth used to wrap a body for burial
2. A thicket; small woods
3. Twist together
4. Noisy
5. Suffering from aches in the muscles, joints, or bones
6. Spoken or carried out with little preparation
7. Show contempt for
8. Having no unique markings; can't be clearly seen
9. Deterioration of mental faculties; senility
10. Verbal expression in speech or writing
11. Unprincipled, crafty acts
12. Ability or power to decide responsibly
13. Wreath or garland for the head
14. To reproach
15. Ghost or soul
16. Gladness; gaiety

A=	B=	C=	D=
E=	F=	G=	H=
I=	J=	K=	L=
M=	N=	O=	P=

Midsummer Night's Dream Vocabulary Magic Squares 3 Answer Key

Match the definition with the vocabulary word. Put your answers in the magic squares below. When your answers are correct, all columns and rows will add to the same number.

A. SHROUD
B. SPRITE
C. UNDISTINGUISHABLE
D. DISCOURSE
E. CLAMOROUS
F. UPBRAID
G. RHEUMATIC
H. KNAVERY
I. CHAPLET
J. ENTWIST
K. DISCRETION
L. EXTEMPORE
M. MIRTH
N. BRAKE
O. DOTAGE
P. FLOUT

1. Cloth used to wrap a body for burial
2. A thicket; small woods
3. Twist together
4. Noisy
5. Suffering from aches in the muscles, joints, or bones
6. Spoken or carried out with little preparation
7. Show contempt for
8. Having no unique markings; can't be clearly seen
9. Deterioration of mental faculties; senility
10. Verbal expression in speech or writing
11. Unprincipled, crafty acts
12. Ability or power to decide responsibly
13. Wreath or garland for the head
14. To reproach
15. Ghost or soul
16. Gladness; gaiety

A=1	B=15	C=8	D=10
E=4	F=14	G=5	H=11
I=13	J=3	K=12	L=6
M=16	N=2	O=9	P=7

Midsummer Night's Dream Vocabulary Magic Squares 4

Match the definition with the vocabulary word. Put your answers in the magic squares below. When your answers are correct, all columns and rows will add to the same number.

A. KINDRED
B. EXTEMPORE
C. AMOROUS
D. REBUKE
E. ENTWIST
F. UPBRAID

G. LOATH
H. BROACHED
I. BOWER
J. TARRYING
K. CHAPLET
L. VISAGE

M. AMIABLE
N. PERJURED
O. ENMITY
P. RECOUNT

1. Friendly and agreeable; good-natured
2. To reproach
3. Pierced in order to draw off liquid
4. Deep-seated, often mutual, hatred
5. Face; appearance
6. Strongly attracted or disposed to love
7. Relating to family
8. Remaining temporarily
9. Wreath or garland for the head
10. Criticize or reprimand
11. Spoken or carried out with little preparation
12. Woman's private chamber in a medieval castle
13. Testified falsely under oath; falsified; untrue
14. Twist together
15. Unwilling or reluctant
16. Narrate the facts or details of

A=	B=	C=	D=
E=	F=	G=	H=
I=	J=	K=	L=
M=	N=	O=	P=

Midsummer Night's Dream Vocabulary Magic Squares 4 Answer Key

Match the definition with the vocabulary word. Put your answers in the magic squares below. When your answers are correct, all columns and rows will add to the same number.

A. KINDRED
B. EXTEMPORE
C. AMOROUS
D. REBUKE
E. ENTWIST
F. UPBRAID
G. LOATH
H. BROACHED
I. BOWER
J. TARRYING
K. CHAPLET
L. VISAGE
M. AMIABLE
N. PERJURED
O. ENMITY
P. RECOUNT

1. Friendly and agreeable; good-natured
2. To reproach
3. Pierced in order to draw off liquid
4. Deep-seated, often mutual, hatred
5. Face; appearance
6. Strongly attracted or disposed to love
7. Relating to family
8. Remaining temporarily
9. Wreath or garland for the head
10. Criticize or reprimand
11. Spoken or carried out with little preparation
12. Woman's private chamber in a medieval castle
13. Testified falsely under oath; falsified; untrue
14. Twist together
15. Unwilling or reluctant
16. Narrate the facts or details of

A=7	B=11	C=6	D=10
E=14	F=2	G=15	H=3
I=12	J=8	K=9	L=5
M=1	N=13	O=4	P=16

Midsummer Night's Dream Vocabulary Word Search 1

```
D O T A G E S D E R D N I K E S A B P C
Z I G P H S E G Q E L B F T U P E R E S
U P S X R R J B M W G P U O Z R X O R H
P P N C O O Y Z C O W O R V R I T A J H
P T B M O R M I S B L O A T H T E C U M
V U A R E U T O S F M B Q V T E M H R J
R N R V A A R P N A J L T A R L P E E R
E E A G M I P S L T P P A L I P O D D L
J N V U E J D C E J O E R O M A R I C L
K B E E B Y D A M M M R R Y H E S R T
T H E X N E J V U P T F Y S M C C L Y
R R D G H U K I B D P O I W U N R R H L
D K L C U Z E S X P A R N N C A T E W K
L V L F Q I J A L M Y C G A W M S T K D
G I X P P Y L G Y V W E I N B G L I V M
F T G D T N C E J C M B X O K J P O O T
R D S J S X W Y D L Q C W Q U R U N L N
R J K L I B X R B M S H S T E S X R T T
N V C T W G D B E R V I K B F H Y H E D
T L Q Q T P L Z Z C A N U H X T M Y U N
L A M E N T A B L E O K A M I A B L E T
V G H R E F J M B Y E U E M V B C W E H
C O N S E C R A T E D V N J L E X R N Z
S P U R N S H R O U D E V T T T F S L S
```

A thicket; small woods (5)
Ability or power to decide responsibly (10)
Bold, insolent, spirited, or original (9)
Bravery; courage (5)
By necessity; by force of circumstances (8)
Cloth used to wrap a body for burial (6)
Criticize or reprimand (6)
Deep-seated, often mutual, hatred (6)
Deluded; cheated; diverted (8)
Deterioration of mental faculties; senility (6)
Face; appearance (6)
Friendly and agreeable; good-natured (7)
Ghost or soul (6)
Give up; abstain from (6)
Gladness; gaiety (5)
High ridge of land jutting out into water (10)
Income; wealth; money (7)
Inspired with love; captivated (8)
Kick at or tread on disdainfully (5)
Narrate the facts or details of (7)
Narrow opening; a crack (5)
Noisy (9)
Pierced in order to draw off liquid (8)
Pleasing to the ear; melodious (6)

Relating to family (7)
Remaining temporarily (8)
Remove (impurities) by or as if by cleansing (5)
Sacred (11)
Show contempt for (5)
Snitched; stole (7)
Spoken or carried out with little preparation (9)
Strongly attracted or disposed to love (7)
Strongly held opinion; conviction (10)
Suffering from aches in the muscles, joints, or bones (9)
Testified falsely under oath; falsified; untrue (8)
The lowest or bottom part (4)
To reproach (7)
Twist together (7)
Unprincipled, crafty acts (7)
Unwilling or reluctant (5)
Verbal expression in speech or writing (9)
Woman's private chamber in a medieval castle (5)
Worry (4)
Worthy of grief, mourning, or regret (10)
Wreath or garland for the head (7)

Midsummer Night's Dream Vocabulary Word Search 1 Answer Key

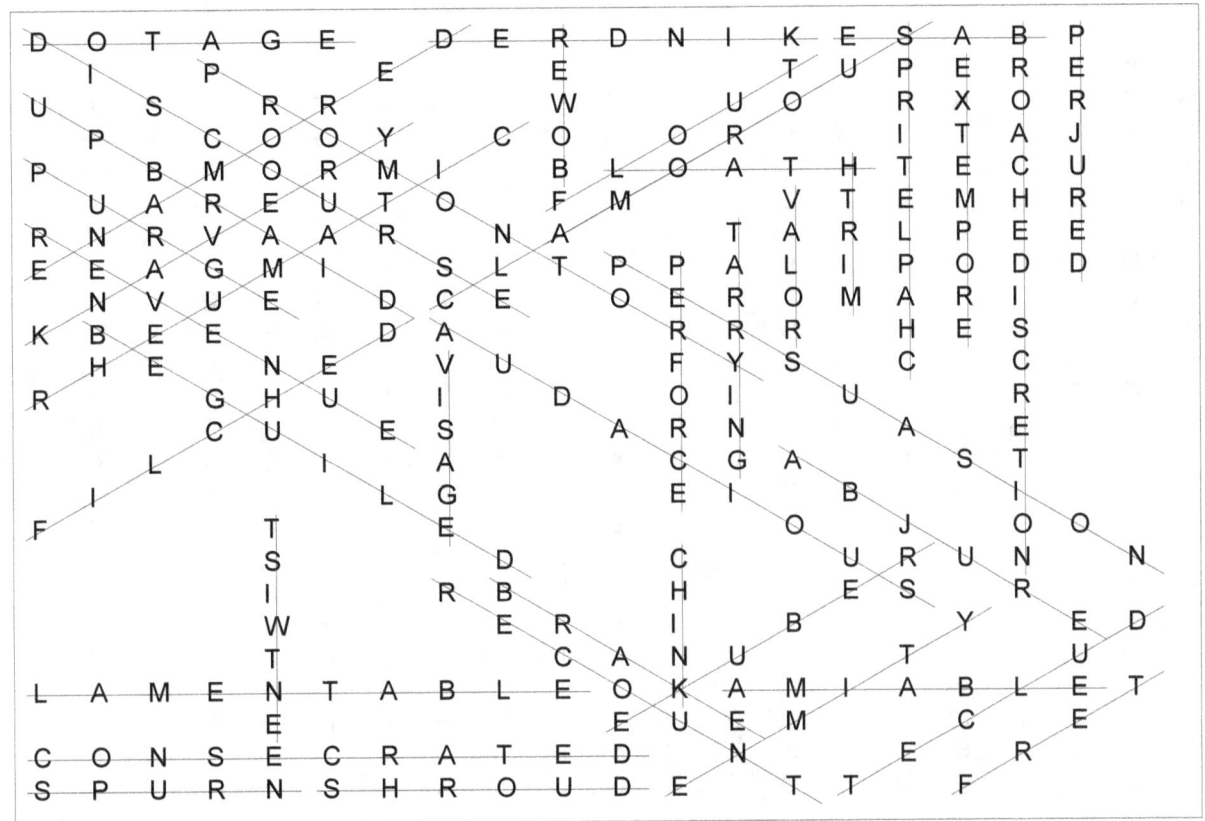

A thicket; small woods (5)
Ability or power to decide responsibly (10)
Bold, insolent, spirited, or original (9)
Bravery; courage (5)
By necessity; by force of circumstances (8)
Cloth used to wrap a body for burial (6)
Criticize or reprimand (6)
Deep-seated, often mutual, hatred (6)
Deluded; cheated; diverted (8)
Deterioration of mental faculties; senility (6)
Face; appearance (6)
Friendly and agreeable; good-natured (7)
Ghost or soul (6)
Give up; abstain from (6)
Gladness; gaiety (5)
High ridge of land jutting out into water (10)
Income; wealth; money (7)
Inspired with love; captivated (8)
Kick at or tread on disdainfully (5)
Narrate the facts or details of (7)
Narrow opening; a crack (5)
Noisy (9)
Pierced in order to draw off liquid (8)
Pleasing to the ear; melodious (6)

Relating to family (7)
Remaining temporarily (8)
Remove (impurities) by or as if by cleansing (5)
Sacred (11)
Show contempt for (5)
Snitched; stole (7)
Spoken or carried out with little preparation (9)
Strongly attracted or disposed to love (7)
Strongly held opinion; conviction (10)
Suffering from aches in the muscles, joints, or bones (9)
Testified falsely under oath; falsified; untrue (8)
The lowest or bottom part (4)
To reproach (7)
Twist together (7)
Unprincipled, crafty acts (7)
Unwilling or reluctant (5)
Verbal expression in speech or writing (9)
Woman's private chamber in a medieval castle (5)
Worry (4)
Worthy of grief, mourning, or regret (10)
Wreath or garland for the head (7)

Midsummer Night's Dream Vocabulary Word Search 2

```
Z P H E L B A H S I U G N I T S I D N U
H K Q X G M L X S L A M E N T A B L E C
H D E T A R C E S N O C A N P M S R A T
N F P E R F O R C E H M S T A G T C B N
X V W M H V D T H Z I D L P L M C R J D
B W V P M I Z E N A S O Y O U I O W U Y
N B F O A Y X C B D Q T N P A R V R R Y
S U O R O M A L C C H A P L E T N S E S
K D B E E Z E U V J U G Y K N H H G V D
J P B P B T Y D X D D E U U T R R V E V
U C D X C E W S A L Q B O X O U W A N F
N O D X E H G C B M E C G U P Y Y L U S
F N M S S S I U J R E C D H R R T O E K
I J K T R O P N I R A Q X O N E T R D D
L U C B U W D R K L C K T F C V W K I K
C N L S O G N F I B E N E L X A P I S Z
H C J Q C Y Y A M T O D B O Q N E N C M
E T M P S T S M E M E V Y U P K R D R C
D I M P I F Q O O N V F J T B W J R E T
Y O F M D Y L R Y R T I H A Q C U E T D
Z N N D F D P O C E X W S Z C M R D I Y
B E C H M S F U P W J E I A L K E R O V
N P E R S U A S I O N H S S G N D W N Z
B R O A C H E D Q B S N D X T E Y V F W
```

A thicket; small woods (5)
Ability or power to decide responsibly (10)
Bold, insolent, spirited, or original (9)
Bravery; courage (5)
By necessity; by force of circumstances (8)
Cloth used to wrap a body for burial (6)
Criticize or reprimand (6)
Deep-seated, often mutual, hatred (6)
Deluded; cheated; diverted (8)
Deterioration of mental faculties; senility (6)
Face; appearance (6)
Friendly and agreeable; good-natured (7)
Ghost or soul (6)
Give up; abstain from (6)
Gladness; gaiety (5)
Having no unique markings; can't be clearly seen (17)
High ridge of land jutting out into water (10)
Income; wealth; money (7)
Inspired with love; captivated (8)
Joint or simultaneous occurrence; done together (11)
Kick at or tread on disdainfully (5)
Narrate the facts or details of (7)

Narrow opening; a crack (5)
Noisy (9)
Pierced in order to draw off liquid (8)
Pleasing to the ear; melodious (6)
Relating to family (7)
Remove (impurities) by or as if by cleansing (5)
Sacred (11)
Show contempt for (5)
Snitched; stole (7)
Spoken or carried out with little preparation (9)
Strongly attracted or disposed to love (7)
Strongly held opinion; conviction (10)
Testified falsely under oath; falsified; untrue (8)
The lowest or bottom part (4)
To reproach (7)
Twist together (7)
Unprincipled, crafty acts (7)
Unwilling or reluctant (5)
Verbal expression in speech or writing (9)
Woman's private chamber in a medieval castle (5)
Worry (4)
Worthy of grief, mourning, or regret (10)
Wreath or garland for the head (7)

Midsummer Night's Dream Vocabulary Word Search 2 Answer Key

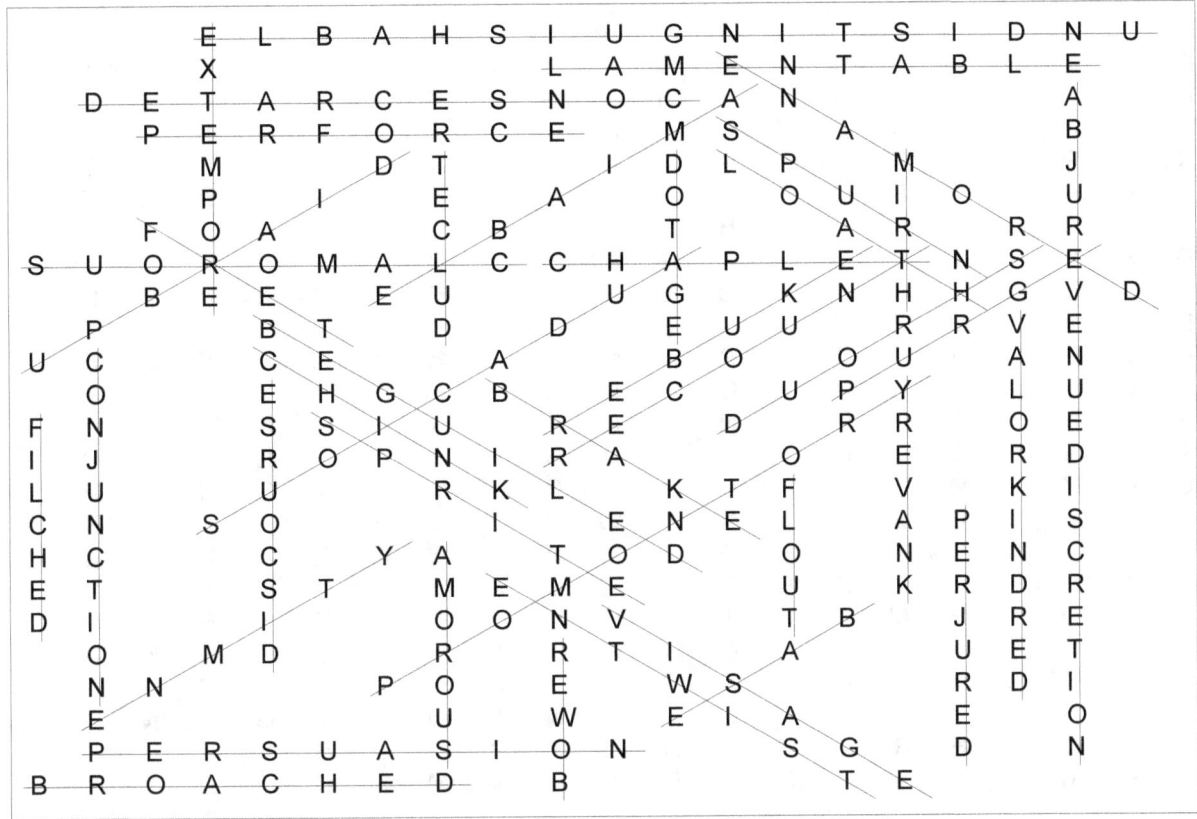

A thicket; small woods (5)
Ability or power to decide responsibly (10)
Bold, insolent, spirited, or original (9)
Bravery; courage (5)
By necessity; by force of circumstances (8)
Cloth used to wrap a body for burial (6)
Criticize or reprimand (6)
Deep-seated, often mutual, hatred (6)
Deluded; cheated; diverted (8)
Deterioration of mental faculties; senility (6)
Face; appearance (6)
Friendly and agreeable; good-natured (7)
Ghost or soul (6)
Give up; abstain from (6)
Gladness; gaiety (5)
Having no unique markings; can't be clearly seen (17)
High ridge of land jutting out into water (10)
Income; wealth; money (7)
Inspired with love; captivated (8)
Joint or simultaneous occurrence; done together (11)
Kick at or tread on disdainfully (5)
Narrate the facts or details of (7)

Narrow opening; a crack (5)
Noisy (9)
Pierced in order to draw off liquid (8)
Pleasing to the ear; melodious (6)
Relating to family (7)
Remove (impurities) by or as if by cleansing (5)
Sacred (11)
Show contempt for (5)
Snitched; stole (7)
Spoken or carried out with little preparation (9)
Strongly attracted or disposed to love (7)
Strongly held opinion; conviction (10)
Testified falsely under oath; falsified; untrue (8)
The lowest or bottom part (4)
To reproach (7)
Twist together (7)
Unprincipled, crafty acts (7)
Unwilling or reluctant (5)
Verbal expression in speech or writing (9)
Woman's private chamber in a medieval castle (5)
Worry (4)
Worthy of grief, mourning, or regret (10)
Wreath or garland for the head (7)

Midsummer Night's Dream Vocabulary Word Search 3

```
N H S X D K G D R P B Z Z S E R F N D H
F S P N N T N R T E T V M F N E R V I J
D K F E Q M D A G M C G L Y T B E W S V
F S P U R N L V V A L O R P W U T E C R
K L P S Z F R S W E A V U X I K L L O G
I P O R T B O R B T R S S N S E A B U K
N V U U I K Y R H T N Y H G T M M A R K
D K B R T T O F C G A M O R O U S I S T
R S M N G A E L Q E M D L R O R B M E L
E B V K C E Q M C T F A O Y B U R A Q C
D L P H V G S W R I M U R R K O D Y Z B
A Q E G A S I V L E S A B N E N W C P R
B D R X B Q V C N N R R I R O V I E E V
J U S L T L H T C M D H Z I A T E P R D
U L U Q W E A R F I C O T W A K D N J P
R C A Q D B M B N T W C T M P I E O U K
E E S K L T J P D Y N N U A A Q Z I R E
N T I E C W K R O U M E Z R G L W T E S
G X O T H M Q X J R H S B C P E R E D V
N J N T A Z K N B R E P T V V T H R K M
G Y R B P S O B E G U I L E D P J C G F
H I H L L C P R O M O N T O R Y G S N S
M Z C D E R O M A N E T R L C S Y I B Y
F P M W T A R R Y I N G M M B S T D T Y
```

ABJURE	CONJUNCTION	FRET	REBUKE
AMIABLE	DISCOURSE	KINDRED	RECOUNT
AMOROUS	DISCRETION	KNAVERY	REVENUE
BASE	DOTAGE	LAMENTABLE	RHEUMATIC
BEGUILED	DULCET	LOATH	SHROUD
BOWER	ENAMORED	MIRTH	SPRITE
BRAKE	ENMITY	PERFORCE	SPURN
BROACHED	ENTWIST	PERJURED	TARRYING
CHAPLET	EXTEMPORE	PERSUASION	UPBRAID
CHINK	FILCHED	PROMONTORY	VALOR
CLAMOROUS	FLOUT	PURGE	VISAGE

Midsummer Night's Dream Vocabulary Word Search 3 Answer Key

ABJURE	CONJUNCTION	FRET	REBUKE
AMIABLE	DISCOURSE	KINDRED	RECOUNT
AMOROUS	DISCRETION	KNAVERY	REVENUE
BASE	DOTAGE	LAMENTABLE	RHEUMATIC
BEGUILED	DULCET	LOATH	SHROUD
BOWER	ENAMORED	MIRTH	SPRITE
BRAKE	ENMITY	PERFORCE	SPURN
BROACHED	ENTWIST	PERJURED	TARRYING
CHAPLET	EXTEMPORE	PERSUASION	UPBRAID
CHINK	FILCHED	PROMONTORY	VALOR
CLAMOROUS	FLOUT	PURGE	VISAGE

Midsummer Night's Dream Vocabulary Word Search 4

```
A B J U R E W O B A S E N A M O R E D D
H B Q A H F N S J L N G N R J Z S G E Y
V M R M E Q R X H M E R K T F R X A H F
S H R O U D Y E I E X U I P W X W T C D
U D Y R M N S T T L T P N E D I L O A K
P X B O A B Y J R B E C D R R T S D O L
B C B U T K L O B A M O R J Q A L T R J
R H T S I F L O U T P N E U W R O G B T
A I M R C A L S L N O S D R B R A P W B
I N Q I V Z P S Z E R E W E Q Y T R X G
D K S P R I T E F M E C B D W I H O F Z
C C Y A M T X G J A C R D V P N V M N D
L R C U R Z H X B L N A J X K G G O R M
A H O D J F K W L O Y T W Q K R F N C Q
M F N A P Y P R I R D E V W D M D T H S
O F J C F G J T E E Y D I I F Y N O A D
R W U I W D E V H B M D S F N U C R P L
O W N O P R A C E S U C A Q O S W Y L L
U K C U C N L L Y P O K G C Z X G F E P
S R T S K I B E G U I L E D U L C E T D
C G I K F A M R R M R E V E N U E X V
Q D O J I Z G S A N P E R F O R C E B F
R H N M B J E T Y K P E R S U A S I O N
Z B A J L S S G B W E Z G C W B M T P K
```

ABJURE	CONJUNCTION	FRET	RECOUNT
AMIABLE	CONSECRATED	KINDRED	REVENUE
AMOROUS	DISCOURSE	KNAVERY	RHEUMATIC
AUDACIOUS	DISCRETION	LAMENTABLE	SHROUD
BASE	DOTAGE	LOATH	SPRITE
BEGUILED	DULCET	MIRTH	SPURN
BOWER	ENAMORED	PERFORCE	TARRYING
BRAKE	ENMITY	PERJURED	UPBRAID
BROACHED	ENTWIST	PERSUASION	VALOR
CHAPLET	EXTEMPORE	PROMONTORY	VISAGE
CHINK	FILCHED	PURGE	
CLAMOROUS	FLOUT	REBUKE	

Midsummer Night's Dream Vocabulary Word Search 4 Answer Key

ABJURE	CONJUNCTION	FRET	RECOUNT
AMIABLE	CONSECRATED	KINDRED	REVENUE
AMOROUS	DISCOURSE	KNAVERY	RHEUMATIC
AUDACIOUS	DISCRETION	LAMENTABLE	SHROUD
BASE	DOTAGE	LOATH	SPRITE
BEGUILED	DULCET	MIRTH	SPURN
BOWER	ENAMORED	PERFORCE	TARRYING
BRAKE	ENMITY	PERJURED	UPBRAID
BROACHED	ENTWIST	PERSUASION	VALOR
CHAPLET	EXTEMPORE	PROMONTORY	VISAGE
CHINK	FILCHED	PURGE	
CLAMOROUS	FLOUT	REBUKE	

Midsummer Night's Dream Vocabulary Crossword 1

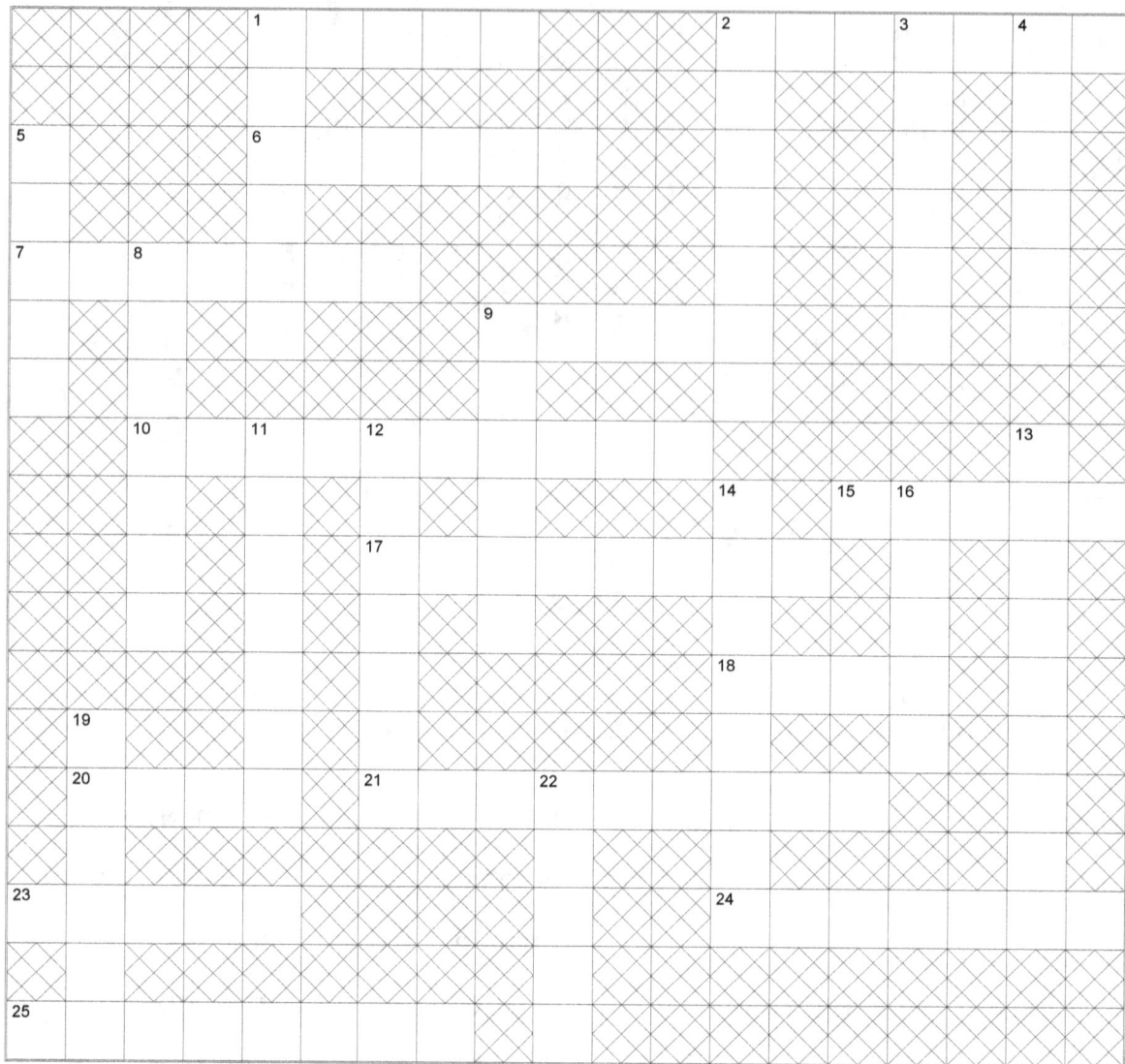

Across
1. Kick at or tread on disdainfully
2. Relating to family
6. Criticize or reprimand
7. Narrate the facts or details of
9. Bravery; courage
10. Strongly held opinion; conviction
15. Show contempt for
17. Deluded; cheated; diverted
18. Worry
20. The lowest or bottom part
21. Verbal expression in speech or writing
23. Remove (impurities) by or as if by cleansing
24. Twist together
25. Testified falsely under oath; falsified; untrue

Down
1. Cloth used to wrap a body for burial
2. Unprincipled, crafty acts
3. Pleasing to the ear; melodious
4. Deep-seated, often mutual, hatred
5. Gladness; gaiety
8. Wreath or garland for the head
9. Face; appearance
11. Income; wealth; money
12. To reproach
13. Bold, insolent, spirited, or original
14. By necessity; by force of circumstances
16. Unwilling or reluctant
19. Give up; abstain from
22. Narrow opening; a crack

Midsummer Night's Dream Vocabulary Crossword 1 Answer Key

			1 S	P	U	R	N		2 K	I	3 N	D	4 R	E	D
			H						N		U		E		N
5 M			6 R	E	B	U	K	E			L		C		M
I			O						A						I
			O						V		C		I		
7 R	E	8 C	O	U	N	T			E		E		T		
T		H					9 V	A	L	O	R		Y		
H		A	D				I		Y						
		10 P	11 E	12 R	S	U	A	S	I	O	N			13 A	
		L		E		P		A		14 P	15 F	16 L	O	U	T
		E		V		17 B	E	G	U	I	L	E	D		D
		T		E		R		E		R		O		A	
				N		A				18 F	R	E	T		C
		19 A		U		I				O		H		I	
		20 B	A	S	E		21 D	I	S	22 C	O	U	R	S	E
		J								H				O	
		23 P	U	R	G	E			I		24 E	N	T	W	I	S	T
		R							N						
25 P	E	R	J	U	R	E	D		K						

Across
1. Kick at or tread on disdainfully
2. Relating to family
6. Criticize or reprimand
7. Narrate the facts or details of
9. Bravery; courage
10. Strongly held opinion; conviction
15. Show contempt for
17. Deluded; cheated; diverted
18. Worry
20. The lowest or bottom part
21. Verbal expression in speech or writing
23. Remove (impurities) by or as if by cleansing
24. Twist together
25. Testified falsely under oath; falsified; untrue

Down
1. Cloth used to wrap a body for burial
2. Unprincipled, crafty acts
3. Pleasing to the ear; melodious
4. Deep-seated, often mutual, hatred
5. Gladness; gaiety
8. Wreath or garland for the head
9. Face; appearance
11. Income; wealth; money
12. To reproach
13. Bold, insolent, spirited, or original
14. By necessity; by force of circumstances
16. Unwilling or reluctant
19. Give up; abstain from
22. Narrow opening; a crack

Midsummer Night's Dream Vocabulary Crossword 2

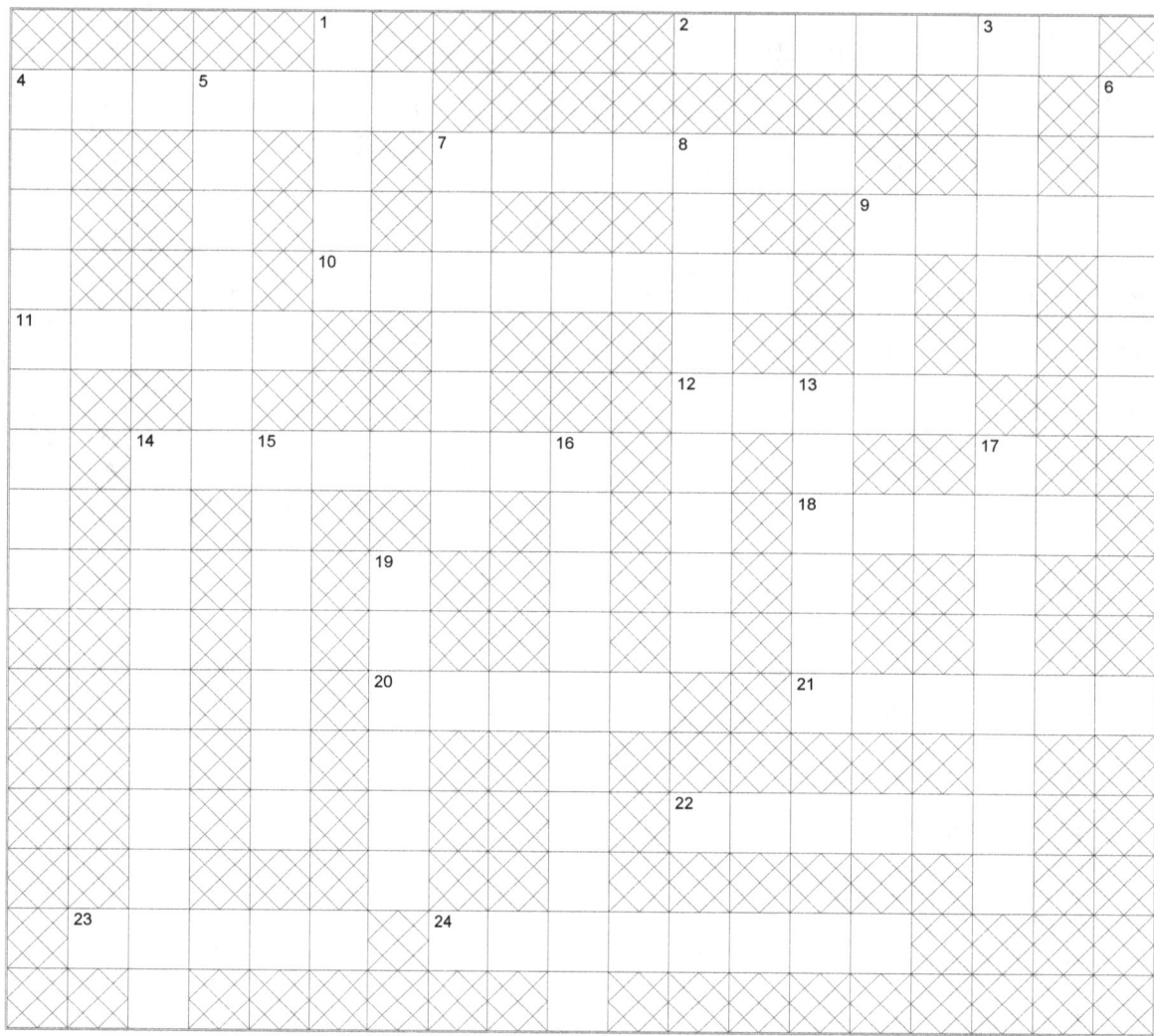

Across
2. Twist together
4. Strongly attracted or disposed to love
7. Relating to family
9. Show contempt for
10. Inspired with love; captivated
11. Narrow opening; a crack
12. Gladness; gaiety
14. Testified falsely under oath; falsified; untrue
18. Woman's private chamber in a medieval castle
20. Kick at or tread on disdainfully
21. Deep-seated, often mutual, hatred
22. Ghost or soul
23. A thicket; small woods
24. Pierced in order to draw off liquid

Down
1. Remove (impurities) by or as if by cleansing
3. Cloth used to wrap a body for burial
4. Bold, insolent, spirited, or original
5. Income; wealth; money
6. Deterioration of mental faculties; senility
7. Unprincipled, crafty acts
8. Suffering from aches in the muscles, joints, or bones
9. Worry
13. Criticize or reprimand
14. High ridge of land jutting out into water
15. Narrate the facts or details of
16. Ability or power to decide responsibly
17. Deluded; cheated; diverted
19. Face; appearance

Midsummer Night's Dream Vocabulary Crossword 2 Answer Key

	1		2			3	
	P		E N T W I S T			S	
4 A M O R 5 O U S						H	6 D
U	E	R	7 K I N D R 8 E D			R	O
D	V	G	N		H		9 F L O U T
A	E	10 E N A M O R E D				R	U	A
11 C H I N K			V		U		E	D	G
I		U		E	12 M I 13 R T H			E
O	14 P E R 15 J U R E 16 D					A		E	17 B
U	R	E		Y		I	18 B O W E R
S	O	C	19 V		S		I	U		G	
	M		O	I		C		C	K		U
	20 O U		S P U R N			21 E N M I T Y
	N	N	A		E			L	
	T	T	G		T	22 S P R I T E
	O		E		I			D
23 B R A K E				24 B R O A C H E D				
	Y			N				

Across
2. Twist together
4. Strongly attracted or disposed to love
7. Relating to family
9. Show contempt for
10. Inspired with love; captivated
11. Narrow opening; a crack
12. Gladness; gaiety
14. Testified falsely under oath; falsified; untrue
18. Woman's private chamber in a medieval castle
20. Kick at or tread on disdainfully
21. Deep-seated, often mutual, hatred
22. Ghost or soul
23. A thicket; small woods
24. Pierced in order to draw off liquid

Down
1. Remove (impurities) by or as if by cleansing
3. Cloth used to wrap a body for burial
4. Bold, insolent, spirited, or original
5. Income; wealth; money
6. Deterioration of mental faculties; senility
7. Unprincipled, crafty acts
8. Suffering from aches in the muscles, joints, or bones
9. Worry
13. Criticize or reprimand
14. High ridge of land jutting out into water
15. Narrate the facts or details of
16. Ability or power to decide responsibly
17. Deluded; cheated; diverted
19. Face; appearance

Midsummer Night's Dream Vocabulary Crossword 3

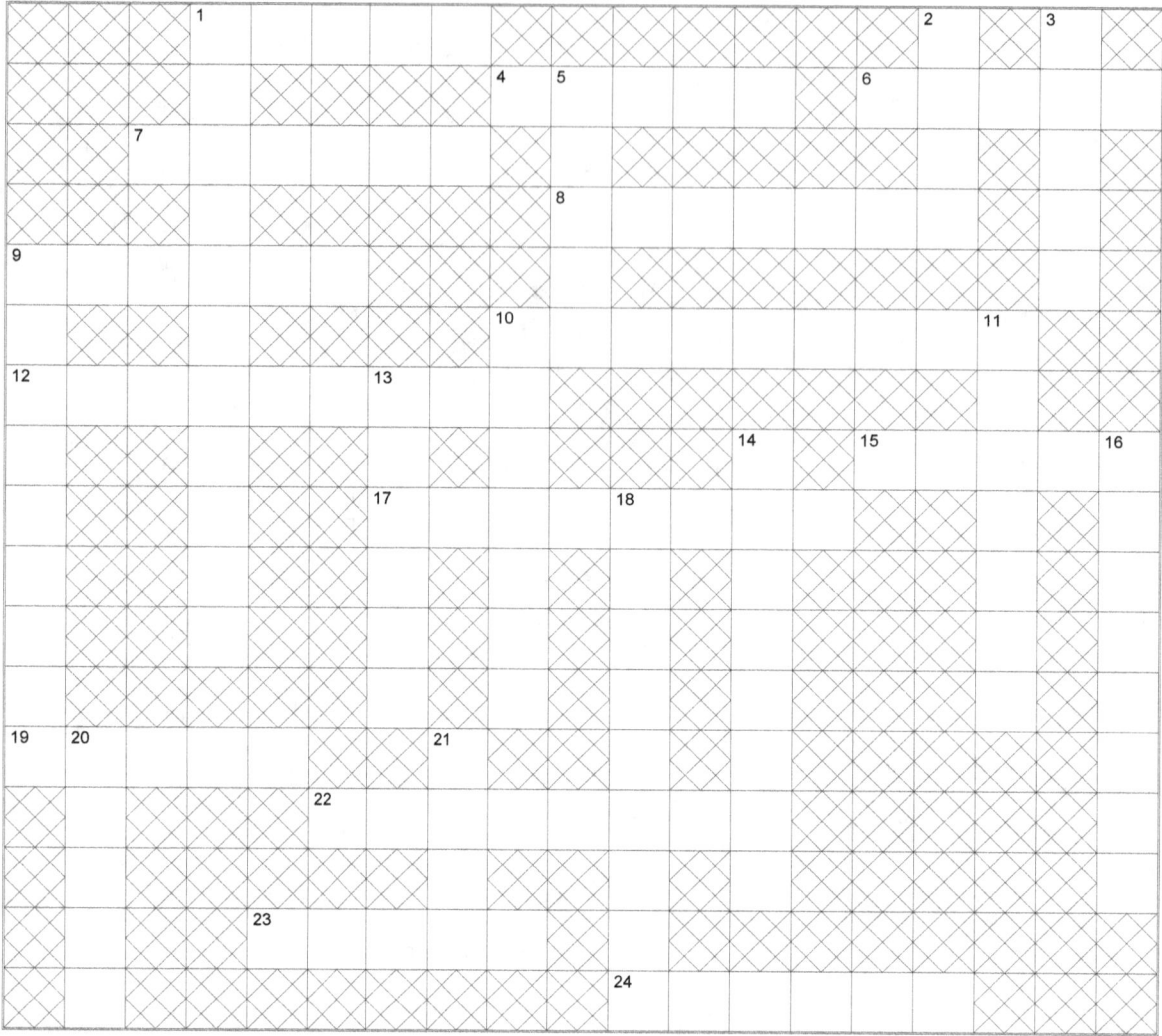

Across
1. Narrow opening; a crack
4. Show contempt for
6. Bravery; courage
7. Deep-seated, often mutual, hatred
8. Friendly and agreeable; good-natured
9. Give up; abstain from
10. Suffering from aches in the muscles, joints, or bones
12. Verbal expression in speech or writing
15. A thicket; small woods
17. Pierced in order to draw off liquid
19. Kick at or tread on disdainfully
22. By necessity; by force of circumstances
23. Gladness; gaiety
24. Cloth used to wrap a body for burial

Down
1. Joint or simultaneous occurrence; done together
2. The lowest or bottom part
3. Woman's private chamber in a medieval castle
5. Unwilling or reluctant
9. Bold, insolent, spirited, or original
10. Narrate the facts or details of
11. Wreath or garland for the head
13. Criticize or reprimand
14. Testified falsely under oath; falsified; untrue
16. Inspired with love; captivated
18. Noisy
20. Remove (impurities) by or as if by cleansing
21. Worry

Midsummer Night's Dream Vocabulary Crossword 3 Answer Key

Across
1. Narrow opening; a crack
4. Show contempt for
6. Bravery; courage
7. Deep-seated, often mutual, hatred
8. Friendly and agreeable; good-natured
9. Give up; abstain from
10. Suffering from aches in the muscles, joints, or bones
12. Verbal expression in speech or writing
15. A thicket; small woods
17. Pierced in order to draw off liquid
19. Kick at or tread on disdainfully
22. By necessity; by force of circumstances
23. Gladness; gaiety
24. Cloth used to wrap a body for burial

Down
1. Joint or simultaneous occurrence; done together
2. The lowest or bottom part
3. Woman's private chamber in a medieval castle
5. Unwilling or reluctant
9. Bold, insolent, spirited, or original
10. Narrate the facts or details of
11. Wreath or garland for the head
13. Criticize or reprimand
14. Testified falsely under oath; falsified; untrue
16. Inspired with love; captivated
18. Noisy
20. Remove (impurities) by or as if by cleansing
21. Worry

Midsummer Night's Dream Vocabulary Crossword 4

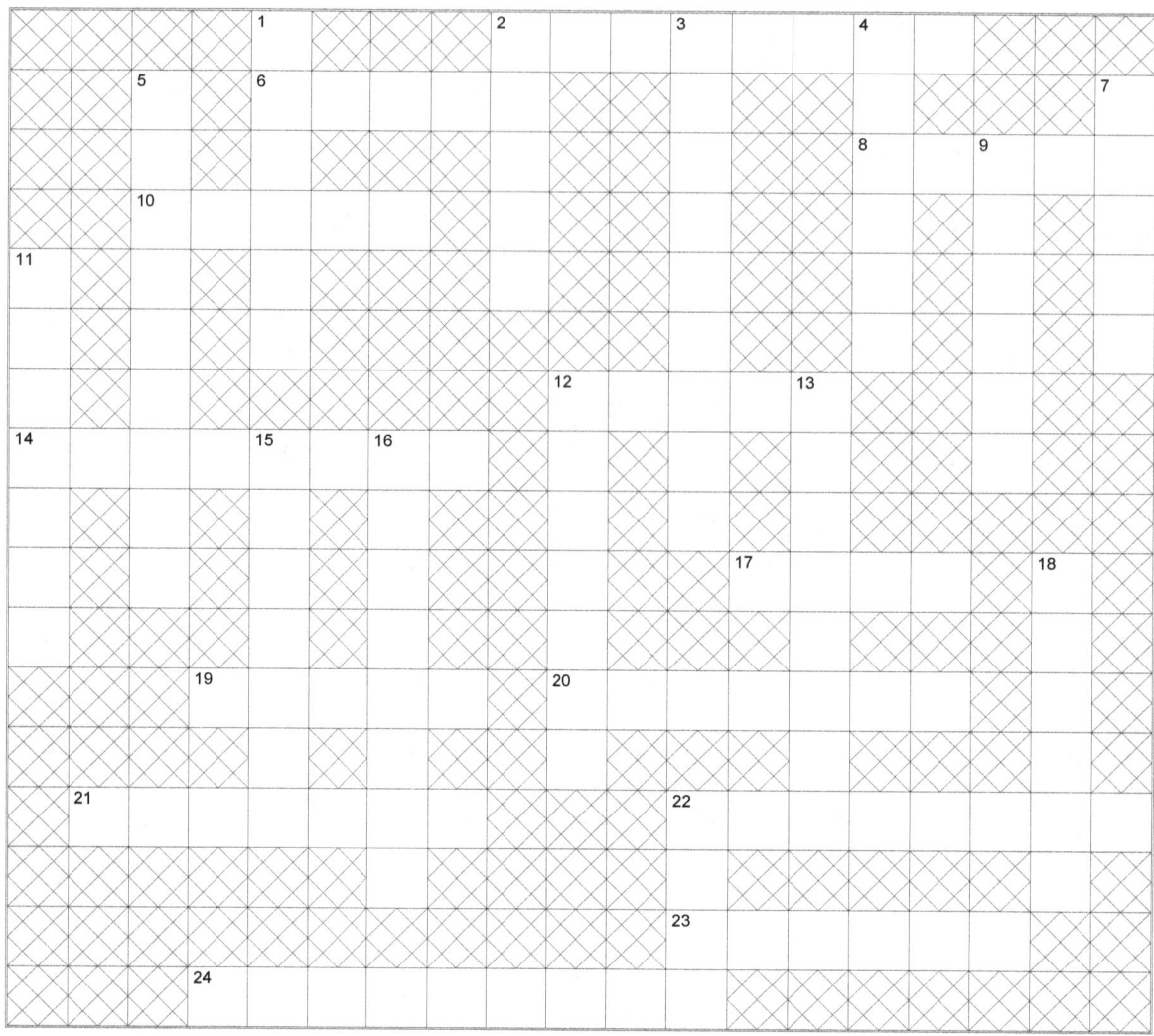

Across
2. Pierced in order to draw off liquid
6. Woman's private chamber in a medieval castle
8. Gladness; gaiety
10. Kick at or tread on disdainfully
12. Show contempt for
14. Testified falsely under oath; falsified; untrue
17. Worry
19. Bravery; courage
20. Twist together
21. Relating to family
22. Deluded; cheated; diverted
23. Cloth used to wrap a body for burial
24. Spoken or carried out with little preparation

Down
1. Give up; abstain from
2. A thicket; small woods
3. Bold, insolent, spirited, or original
4. Deep-seated, often mutual, hatred
5. Verbal expression in speech or writing
7. Narrow opening; a crack
9. Criticize or reprimand
11. Wreath or garland for the head
12. Snitched; stole
13. Remaining temporarily
15. To reproach
16. Inspired with love; captivated
18. Pleasing to the ear; melodious
22. The lowest or bottom part

Midsummer Night's Dream Vocabulary Crossword 4 Answer Key

			1 A			2 B	R	O	3 A	C	H	4 E	D		
		5 D		6 B	O	W	E	R		U		N			7 C
		I		J			A		D			8 M	I	9 R	T	H
			10 S	P	U	R	N		K	A		I		E		I
11 C		C		R			E		C			T		B		N
H		O		E					I		13 T	Y		U		K
A		U				12 F	L	O	U	T				K		
14 P	E	15 R	J	16 U	R	E	D		I		U		A		E	
L		S		P		N			L		S		R			
E		E		B		A			C		17 F	R	E	T	18 D	
T				R		M			H				Y		U	
			19 V	A	L	O	R		20 E	N	T	W	I	S	T	L
				I		R			D			N			C	
		21 K	I	N	D	R	E	D			22 B	E	G	U	I	L	E	D
						D					A				T	
									23 S	H	R	O	U	D		
			24 E	X	T	E	M	P	O	R	E					

Across
2. Pierced in order to draw off liquid
6. Woman's private chamber in a medieval castle
8. Gladness; gaiety
10. Kick at or tread on disdainfully
12. Show contempt for
14. Testified falsely under oath; falsified; untrue
17. Worry
19. Bravery; courage
20. Twist together
21. Relating to family
22. Deluded; cheated; diverted
23. Cloth used to wrap a body for burial
24. Spoken or carried out with little preparation

Down
1. Give up; abstain from
2. A thicket; small woods
3. Bold, insolent, spirited, or original
4. Deep-seated, often mutual, hatred
5. Verbal expression in speech or writing
7. Narrow opening; a crack
9. Criticize or reprimand
11. Wreath or garland for the head
12. Snitched; stole
13. Remaining temporarily
15. To reproach
16. Inspired with love; captivated
18. Pleasing to the ear; melodious
22. The lowest or bottom part

Midsummer Night's Dream Vocabulary Juggle Letters 1

1. CADIUOASU = 1. _____
Bold, insolent, spirited, or original

2. MYITEN = 2. _____
Deep-seated, often mutual, hatred

3. JBEURA = 3. _____
Give up; abstain from

4. ORCAMLUOS = 4. _____
Noisy

5. LUFTO = 5. _____
Show contempt for

6. DTEENRCASOC = 6. _____
Sacred

7. TCONNNUCJOI = 7. _____
Joint or simultaneous occurrence; done together

8. SRUDHO = 8. _____
Cloth used to wrap a body for burial

9. MTIRH = 9. _____
Gladness; gaiety

10. ODRAEMEN =10. _____
Inspired with love; captivated

11. EKUBER =11. _____
Criticize or reprimand

12. SOUMAOR =12. _____
Strongly attracted or disposed to love

13. IVESAG =13. _____
Face; appearance

14. MEEOPERTX =14. _____
Spoken or carried out with little preparation

15. HEATLCP =15. _____
Wreath or garland for the head

Midsummer Night's Dream Vocabulary Juggle Letters 1 Answer Key

1. CADIUOASU = 1. AUDACIOUS
   Bold, insolent, spirited, or original

2. MYITEN = 2. ENMITY
   Deep-seated, often mutual, hatred

3. JBEURA = 3. ABJURE
   Give up; abstain from

4. ORCAMLUOS = 4. CLAMOROUS
   Noisy

5. LUFTO = 5. FLOUT
   Show contempt for

6. DTEENRCASOC = 6. CONSECRATED
   Sacred

7. TCONNNUCJOI = 7. CONJUNCTION
   Joint or simultaneous occurrence; done together

8. SRUDHO = 8. SHROUD
   Cloth used to wrap a body for burial

9. MTIRH = 9. MIRTH
   Gladness; gaiety

10. ODRAEMEN = 10. ENAMORED
    Inspired with love; captivated

11. EKUBER = 11. REBUKE
    Criticize or reprimand

12. SOUMAOR = 12. AMOROUS
    Strongly attracted or disposed to love

13. IVESAG = 13. VISAGE
    Face; appearance

14. MEEOPERTX = 14. EXTEMPORE
    Spoken or carried out with little preparation

15. HEATLCP = 15. CHAPLET
    Wreath or garland for the head

Midsummer Night's Dream Vocabulary Juggle Letters 2

1. CDTLEU = 1. _____
   Pleasing to the ear; melodious

2. RHSUOD = 2. _____
   Cloth used to wrap a body for burial

3. TNIROCESID = 3. _____
   Ability or power to decide responsibly

4. IETPSR = 4. _____
   Ghost or soul

5. RENIDKD = 5. _____
   Relating to family

6. COEFREPR = 6. _____
   By necessity; by force of circumstances

7. BAEUJR = 7. _____
   Give up; abstain from

8. EDRRUPJE = 8. _____
   Testified falsely under oath; falsified; untrue

9. AIDUPRB = 9. _____
   To reproach

10. RPISASNOEU = 10. _____
    Strongly held opinion; conviction

11. AEBS = 11. _____
    The lowest or bottom part

12. NSOETCCADRE = 12. _____
    Sacred

13. OBREW = 13. _____
    Woman's private chamber in a medieval castle

14. ORLAV = 14. _____
    Bravery; courage

15. DAACIUUSO = 15. _____
    Bold, insolent, spirited, or original

Midsummer Night's Dream Vocabulary Juggle Letters 2 Answer Key

1. CDTLEU = 1. DULCET
Pleasing to the ear; melodious

2. RHSUOD = 2. SHROUD
Cloth used to wrap a body for burial

3. TNIROCESID = 3. DISCRETION
Ability or power to decide responsibly

4. IETPSR = 4. SPRITE
Ghost or soul

5. RENIDKD = 5. KINDRED
Relating to family

6. COEFREPR = 6. PERFORCE
By necessity; by force of circumstances

7. BAEUJR = 7. ABJURE
Give up; abstain from

8. EDRRUPJE = 8. PERJURED
Testified falsely under oath; falsified; untrue

9. AIDUPRB = 9. UPBRAID
To reproach

10. RPISASNOEU = 10. PERSUASION
Strongly held opinion; conviction

11. AEBS = 11. BASE
The lowest or bottom part

12. NSOETCCADRE = 12. CONSECRATED
Sacred

13. OBREW = 13. BOWER
Woman's private chamber in a medieval castle

14. ORLAV = 14. VALOR
Bravery; courage

15. DAACIUUSO = 15. AUDACIOUS
Bold, insolent, spirited, or original

Midsummer Night's Dream Vocabulary Juggle Letters 3

1. BEAAILM = 1. _____
   Friendly and agreeable; good-natured

2. KRUBEE = 2. _____
   Criticize or reprimand

3. NSPRU = 3. _____
   Kick at or tread on disdainfully

4. BHSDINUGTIEUNSALI = 4. _____
   Having no unique markings; can't be clearly seen

5. RSPAIOEUSN = 5. _____
   Strongly held opinion; conviction

6. ESBA = 6. _____
   The lowest or bottom part

7. NKCIH = 7. _____
   Narrow opening; a crack

8. VENEURE = 8. _____
   Income; wealth; money

9. TDCUEL = 9. _____
   Pleasing to the ear; melodious

10. NRSTCEOCEDA =10. _____
    Sacred

11. LEPATHC =11. _____
    Wreath or garland for the head

12. AVROL =12. _____
    Bravery; courage

13. HLDCIEF =13. _____
    Snitched; stole

14. GPUER =14. _____
    Remove (impurities) by or as if by cleansing

15. IVASGE =15. _____
    Face; appearance

Midsummer Night's Dream Vocabulary Juggle Letters 3 Answer Key

1. BEAAILM = 1. AMIABLE
   Friendly and agreeable; good-natured

2. KRUBEE = 2. REBUKE
   Criticize or reprimand

3. NSPRU = 3. SPURN
   Kick at or tread on disdainfully

4. BHSDINUGTIEUNSALI = 4. UNDISTINGUISHABLE
   Having no unique markings; can't be clearly seen

5. RSPAIOEUSN = 5. PERSUASION
   Strongly held opinion; conviction

6. ESBA = 6. BASE
   The lowest or bottom part

7. NKCIH = 7. CHINK
   Narrow opening; a crack

8. VENEURE = 8. REVENUE
   Income; wealth; money

9. TDCUEL = 9. DULCET
   Pleasing to the ear; melodious

10. NRSTCEOCEDA =10. CONSECRATED
    Sacred

11. LEPATHC =11. CHAPLET
    Wreath or garland for the head

12. AVROL =12. VALOR
    Bravery; courage

13. HLDCIEF =13. FILCHED
    Snitched; stole

14. GPUER =14. PURGE
    Remove (impurities) by or as if by cleansing

15. IVASGE =15. VISAGE
    Face; appearance

Midsummer Night's Dream Vocabulary Juggle Letters 4

1. EBARK = 1. _____
A thicket; small woods

2. JERDUPER = 2. _____
Testified falsely under oath; falsified; untrue

3. ERTPSI = 3. _____
Ghost or soul

4. ECDORHAB = 4. _____
Pierced in order to draw off liquid

5. OYOOTNRMRP = 5. _____
High ridge of land jutting out into water

6. ERWOB = 6. _____
Woman's private chamber in a medieval castle

7. ETLDCU = 7. _____
Pleasing to the ear; melodious

8. TOGAED = 8. _____
Deterioration of mental faculties; senility

9. EETXMEROP = 9. _____
Spoken or carried out with little preparation

10. URPNS = 10. _____
Kick at or tread on disdainfully

11. AURMLOOCS = 11. _____
Noisy

12. RDAMNOEE = 12. _____
Inspired with love; captivated

13. NREKYVA = 13. _____
Unprincipled, crafty acts

14. CEOREFRP = 14. _____
By necessity; by force of circumstances

15. ROCETNSIDI = 15. _____
Ability or power to decide responsibly

Midsummer Night's Dream Vocabulary Juggle Letters 4 Answer Key

1. EBARK = 1. BRAKE
   A thicket; small woods

2. JERDUPER = 2. PERJURED
   Testified falsely under oath; falsified; untrue

3. ERTPSI = 3. SPRITE
   Ghost or soul

4. ECDORHAB = 4. BROACHED
   Pierced in order to draw off liquid

5. OYOOTNRMRP = 5. PROMONTORY
   High ridge of land jutting out into water

6. ERWOB = 6. BOWER
   Woman's private chamber in a medieval castle

7. ETLDCU = 7. DULCET
   Pleasing to the ear; melodious

8. TOGAED = 8. DOTAGE
   Deterioration of mental faculties; senility

9. EETXMEROP = 9. EXTEMPORE
   Spoken or carried out with little preparation

10. URPNS = 10. SPURN
    Kick at or tread on disdainfully

11. AURMLOOCS = 11. CLAMOROUS
    Noisy

12. RDAMNOEE = 12. ENAMORED
    Inspired with love; captivated

13. NREKYVA = 13. KNAVERY
    Unprincipled, crafty acts

14. CEOREFRP = 14. PERFORCE
    By necessity; by force of circumstances

15. ROCETNSIDI = 15. DISCRETION
    Ability or power to decide responsibly

ABJURE	Give up; abstain from
AMIABLE	Friendly and agreeable; good-natured
AMOROUS	Strongly attracted or disposed to love
AUDACIOUS	Bold, insolent, spirited, or original
BASE	The lowest or bottom part
BEGUILED	Deluded; cheated; diverted

BOWER	Woman's private chamber in a medieval castle
BRAKE	A thicket; small woods
BROACHED	Pierced in order to draw off liquid
CHAPLET	Wreath or garland for the head
CHINK	Narrow opening; a crack
CLAMOROUS	Noisy

CONJUNCTION	Joint or simultaneous occurrence; done together
CONSECRATED	Sacred
DISCOURSE	Verbal expression in speech or writing
DISCRETION	Ability or power to decide responsibly
DOTAGE	Deterioration of mental faculties; senility
DULCET	Pleasing to the ear; melodious

ENAMORED	Inspired with love; captivated
ENMITY	Deep-seated, often mutual, hatred
ENTWIST	Twist together
EXTEMPORE	Spoken or carried out with little preparation
FILCHED	Snitched; stole
FLOUT	Show contempt for

FRET	Worry
KINDRED	Relating to family
KNAVERY	Unprincipled, crafty acts
LAMENTABLE	Worthy of grief, mourning, or regret
LOATH	Unwilling or reluctant
MIRTH	Gladness; gaiety

PERFORCE	By necessity; by force of circumstances
PERJURED	Testified falsely under oath; falsified; untrue
PERSUASION	Strongly held opinion; conviction
PROMONTORY	High ridge of land jutting out into water
PURGE	Remove (impurities) by or as if by cleansing
REBUKE	Criticize or reprimand

RECOUNT	Narrate the facts or details of
REVENUE	Income; wealth; money
RHEUMATIC	Suffering from aches in the muscles, joints, or bones
SHROUD	Cloth used to wrap a body for burial
SPRITE	Ghost or soul
SPURN	Kick at or tread on disdainfully

TARRYING	Remaining temporarily
UNDISTINGUISHABLE	Having no unique markings; can't be clearly seen
UPBRAID	To reproach
VALOR	Bravery; courage
VISAGE	Face; appearance

Midsummer Night's Dream Vocab

RHEUMATIC	BROACHED	ENMITY	REVENUE	TARRYING
UNDISTIN GUISHABLE	FILCHED	CHINK	CONJUNCTION	PROMONTORY
SPRITE	PERSUASION	FREE SPACE	SHROUD	PERFORCE
SPURN	DULCET	BOWER	RECOUNT	BRAKE
ENAMORED	VALOR	AMOROUS	MIRTH	AMIABLE

Midsummer Night's Dream Vocab

CHAPLET	PURGE	VISAGE	LOATH	PERJURED
BEGUILED	CONSECRATED	FLOUT	KNAVERY	DISCOURSE
DOTAGE	EXTEMPORE	FREE SPACE	DISCRETION	BASE
AUDACIOUS	UPBRAID	ENTWIST	CLAMOROUS	LAMENTABLE
FRET	REBUKE	AMIABLE	MIRTH	AMOROUS

Midsummer Night's Dream Vocab

DISCRETION	PERSUASION	REVENUE	DULCET	CONSECRATED
FRET	PERFORCE	CLAMOROUS	BROACHED	RHEUMATIC
PROMONTORY	ENTWIST	FREE SPACE	PERJURED	UPBRAID
DOTAGE	KNAVERY	TARRYING	BRAKE	UNDISTINGUISHABLE
BASE	SPURN	DISCOURSE	RECOUNT	ENMITY

Midsummer Night's Dream Vocab

VISAGE	EXTEMPORE	SHROUD	KINDRED	CHINK
ENAMORED	CHAPLET	AMOROUS	CONJUNCTION	LOATH
PURGE	SPRITE	FREE SPACE	FLOUT	AUDACIOUS
ABJURE	FILCHED	VALOR	MIRTH	LAMENTABLE
AMIABLE	BOWER	ENMITY	RECOUNT	DISCOURSE

Midsummer Night's Dream Vocab

DISCOURSE	KNAVERY	ENMITY	SPRITE	TARRYING
SHROUD	BASE	LAMENTABLE	LOATH	DULCET
MIRTH	PERSUASION	FREE SPACE	EXTEMPORE	DISCRETION
CONJUNCTION	PROMONTORY	SPURN	CHAPLET	PERFORCE
AMIABLE	FILCHED	BROACHED	RECOUNT	AMOROUS

Midsummer Night's Dream Vocab

PURGE	AUDACIOUS	RHEUMATIC	REVENUE	REBUKE
ENAMORED	CONSECRATED	CHINK	BEGUILED	VALOR
FRET	VISAGE	FREE SPACE	UPBRAID	DOTAGE
CLAMOROUS	ABJURE	ENTWIST	BRAKE	UNDISTINGUISHABLE
KINDRED	FLOUT	AMOROUS	RECOUNT	BROACHED

Midsummer Night's Vocab

UNDISTINGUISHABLE	CONJUNCTION	DISCOURSE	FILCHED	DOTAGE
ENTWIST	BRAKE	AMIABLE	PURGE	MIRTH
LAMENTABLE	CONSECRATED	FREE SPACE	DISCRETION	BROACHED
PERSUASION	ENMITY	BOWER	BASE	AMOROUS
PROMONTORY	KINDRED	TARRYING	CHAPLET	ENAMORED

Midsummer Night's Dream Vocab

REVENUE	DULCET	ABJURE	SHROUD	FLOUT
BEGUILED	RHEUMATIC	LOATH	UPBRAID	VALOR
FRET	PERFORCE	FREE SPACE	EXTEMPORE	KNAVERY
SPURN	RECOUNT	PERJURED	VISAGE	AUDACIOUS
CLAMOROUS	REBUKE	ENAMORED	CHAPLET	TARRYING

Midsummer Night's Dream Vocab

DISCRETION	AUDACIOUS	CLAMOROUS	DULCET	PERJURED
REVENUE	SHROUD	FRET	RECOUNT	SPURN
BEGUILED	BOWER	FREE SPACE	REBUKE	UPBRAID
UNDISTINGUISHABLE	PERSUASION	CHAPLET	FLOUT	KNAVERY
PURGE	BASE	AMOROUS	VALOR	SPRITE

Midsummer Night's Dream Vocab

ENTWIST	PERFORCE	DISCOURSE	TARRYING	LOATH
ENAMORED	EXTEMPORE	FILCHED	LAMENTABLE	ABJURE
KINDRED	MIRTH	FREE SPACE	DOTAGE	VISAGE
CONJUNCTION	RHEUMATIC	CHINK	CONSECRATED	AMIABLE
BRAKE	BROACHED	SPRITE	VALOR	AMOROUS

Midsummer Night's Dream Vocab

ENAMORED	AUDACIOUS	REVENUE	SHROUD	DISCOURSE
BOWER	SPRITE	CONSECRATED	UPBRAID	ABJURE
FILCHED	TARRYING	FREE SPACE	BASE	ENTWIST
KNAVERY	EXTEMPORE	CLAMOROUS	BEGUILED	BRAKE
VALOR	AMOROUS	VISAGE	SPURN	RECOUNT

Midsummer Night's Dream Vocab

MIRTH	DISCRETION	LAMENTABLE	AMIABLE	KINDRED
BROACHED	ENMITY	DOTAGE	PERSUASION	CHAPLET
FLOUT	RHEUMATIC	FREE SPACE	UNDISTINGUISHABLE	CHINK
PURGE	PERFORCE	DULCET	PERJURED	FRET
LOATH	PROMONTORY	RECOUNT	SPURN	VISAGE

Midsummer Night's Dream Vocab

UNDISTIN GUISHABLE	MIRTH	AMIABLE	CHAPLET	DULCET
EXTEMPORE	ENAMORED	FRET	BASE	BOWER
PERSUASION	CHINK	FREE SPACE	REBUKE	VALOR
UPBRAID	LAMENTABLE	ABJURE	AMOROUS	CONSECRATED
PROMONTORY	KNAVERY	KINDRED	REVENUE	BRAKE

Midsummer Night's Dream Vocab

AUDACIOUS	ENTWIST	VISAGE	DOTAGE	PERFORCE
ENMITY	SPURN	DISCOURSE	RECOUNT	TARRYING
BROACHED	BEGUILED	FREE SPACE	FLOUT	CONJUNCTION
DISCRETION	LOATH	SPRITE	RHEUMATIC	CLAMOROUS
PERJURED	PURGE	BRAKE	REVENUE	KINDRED

Midsummer Night's Dream Vocab

ENTWIST	FRET	PERJURED	CLAMOROUS	REBUKE
VISAGE	ENAMORED	TARRYING	UPBRAID	SHROUD
ABJURE	VALOR	FREE SPACE	CONSECRATED	RHEUMATIC
LAMENTABLE	PROMONTORY	AMOROUS	PURGE	CHINK
KINDRED	SPURN	BOWER	BASE	BROACHED

Midsummer Night's Dream Vocab

DOTAGE	ENMITY	FLOUT	UNDISTINGUISHABLE	BRAKE
MIRTH	DULCET	DISCOURSE	KNAVERY	RECOUNT
CONJUNCTION	PERFORCE	FREE SPACE	AUDACIOUS	FILCHED
DISCRETION	AMIABLE	REVENUE	PERSUASION	SPRITE
BEGUILED	CHAPLET	BROACHED	BASE	BOWER

Midsummer Night's Dream Vocab

UPBRAID	ENTWIST	BASE	AMIABLE	RHEUMATIC
SPRITE	MIRTH	BRAKE	PURGE	REVENUE
FRET	CLAMOROUS	FREE SPACE	KNAVERY	UNDISTINGUISHABLE
CHINK	DISCOURSE	AMOROUS	RECOUNT	REBUKE
PERJURED	VALOR	LOATH	TARRYING	DOTAGE

Midsummer Night's Dream Vocab

PERSUASION	FLOUT	PERFORCE	FILCHED	KINDRED
SHROUD	LAMENTABLE	CONJUNCTION	SPURN	CHAPLET
ENMITY	AUDACIOUS	FREE SPACE	EXTEMPORE	PROMONTORY
ENAMORED	CONSECRATED	DISCRETION	VISAGE	BROACHED
BEGUILED	DULCET	DOTAGE	TARRYING	LOATH

Midsummer Night's Dream Vocab

BOWER	CONSECRATED	LAMENTABLE	CONJUNCTION	AUDACIOUS
VISAGE	AMIABLE	KINDRED	UPBRAID	ENMITY
EXTEMPORE	MIRTH	FREE SPACE	REBUKE	PROMONTORY
BRAKE	DISCRETION	FILCHED	LOATH	VALOR
TARRYING	AMOROUS	SPURN	FRET	BROACHED

Midsummer Night's Dream Vocab

SPRITE	UNDISTINGUISHABLE	SHROUD	CLAMOROUS	REVENUE
RECOUNT	FLOUT	PURGE	CHAPLET	KNAVERY
DISCOURSE	PERFORCE	FREE SPACE	PERSUASION	DOTAGE
PERJURED	ENAMORED	CHINK	BEGUILED	ENTWIST
DULCET	RHEUMATIC	BROACHED	FRET	SPURN

Midsummer Night's Dream Vocab

AMIABLE	FILCHED	RHEUMATIC	CHAPLET	SPRITE
ENAMORED	ENTWIST	VALOR	LOATH	FLOUT
SHROUD	MIRTH	FREE SPACE	UPBRAID	PERSUASION
AMOROUS	UNDISTIN GUISHABLE	LAMENTABLE	REVENUE	DISCRETION
VISAGE	BEGUILED	FRET	CONJUNCTION	BRAKE

Midsummer Night's Dream Vocab

EXTEMPORE	BASE	AUDACIOUS	REBUKE	KINDRED
PURGE	KNAVERY	SPURN	BROACHED	PERJURED
ENMITY	DULCET	FREE SPACE	RECOUNT	PERFORCE
TARRYING	DISCOURSE	ABJURE	CLAMOROUS	CONSECRATED
BOWER	CHINK	BRAKE	CONJUNCTION	FRET

Midsummer Night's Dream Vocab

AMIABLE	KINDRED	PURGE	RHEUMATIC	AMOROUS
DULCET	EXTEMPORE	CONSECRATED	REBUKE	DISCOURSE
BOWER	PROMONTORY	FREE SPACE	KNAVERY	PERJURED
VISAGE	FLOUT	ENTWIST	UNDISTINGUISHABLE	DISCRETION
ENAMORED	UPBRAID	LOATH	AUDACIOUS	FILCHED

Midsummer Night's Dream Vocab

CLAMOROUS	REVENUE	SHROUD	BRAKE	VALOR
ABJURE	CONJUNCTION	ENMITY	PERSUASION	TARRYING
PERFORCE	MIRTH	FREE SPACE	BROACHED	CHINK
FRET	BEGUILED	RECOUNT	SPURN	LAMENTABLE
BASE	DOTAGE	FILCHED	AUDACIOUS	LOATH

Midsummer Night's Dream Vocab

DULCET	RECOUNT	EXTEMPORE	PURGE	BEGUILED
CHINK	CLAMOROUS	AUDACIOUS	PROMONTORY	ABJURE
BRAKE	CONSECRATED	FREE SPACE	PERSUASION	SPURN
ENAMORED	DISCOURSE	LAMENTABLE	PERFORCE	FLOUT
UPBRAID	BROACHED	KNAVERY	LOATH	CONJUNCTION

Midsummer Night's Dream Vocab

CHAPLET	VISAGE	AMIABLE	RHEUMATIC	VALOR
BOWER	ENTWIST	DOTAGE	REVENUE	TARRYING
FRET	DISCRETION	FREE SPACE	UNDISTIN GUISHABLE	MIRTH
KINDRED	PERJURED	BASE	SPRITE	FILCHED
ENMITY	SHROUD	CONJUNCTION	LOATH	KNAVERY

Midsummer Night's Dream Vocab

FLOUT	CHINK	REBUKE	VISAGE	UPBRAID
DISCOURSE	CONSECRATED	VALOR	PURGE	ABJURE
SHROUD	SPRITE	FREE SPACE	PROMONTORY	KINDRED
KNAVERY	RHEUMATIC	FRET	ENTWIST	SPURN
REVENUE	UNDISTINGUISHABLE	TARRYING	DISCRETION	AMOROUS

Midsummer Night's Dream Vocab

PERJURED	BRAKE	ENMITY	BROACHED	LOATH
EXTEMPORE	RECOUNT	BEGUILED	AUDACIOUS	LAMENTABLE
PERFORCE	BOWER	FREE SPACE	AMIABLE	FILCHED
PERSUASION	CONJUNCTION	BASE	CHAPLET	DULCET
CLAMOROUS	DOTAGE	AMOROUS	DISCRETION	TARRYING

Midsummer Night's Dream Vocab

RECOUNT	CLAMOROUS	SPRITE	ENAMORED	ABJURE
ENTWIST	DISCOURSE	ENMITY	FLOUT	FILCHED
SHROUD	BRAKE	FREE SPACE	PROMONTORY	FRET
AMOROUS	KINDRED	KNAVERY	EXTEMPORE	VISAGE
BROACHED	LOATH	DISCRETION	REVENUE	PERFORCE

Midsummer Night's Dream Vocab

TARRYING	CONJUNCTION	AUDACIOUS	UPBRAID	AMIABLE
VALOR	CHINK	DULCET	LAMENTABLE	SPURN
REBUKE	BASE	FREE SPACE	CONSECRATED	CHAPLET
UNDISTINGUISHABLE	MIRTH	PURGE	DOTAGE	PERJURED
BEGUILED	PERSUASION	PERFORCE	REVENUE	DISCRETION

Midsummer Night's Dream Vocab

ENTWIST	CHAPLET	DULCET	RHEUMATIC	CHINK
LOATH	LAMENTABLE	UNDISTIN GUISHABLE	VALOR	REBUKE
MIRTH	ENAMORED	FREE SPACE	RECOUNT	DOTAGE
ABJURE	SPURN	CLAMOROUS	ENMITY	PERFORCE
TARRYING	VISAGE	EXTEMPORE	FILCHED	AUDACIOUS

Midsummer Night's Dream Vocab

KNAVERY	SHROUD	CONSECRATED	FLOUT	KINDRED
CONJUNCTION	AMOROUS	DISCRETION	FRET	BEGUILED
PERJURED	DISCOURSE	FREE SPACE	PERSUASION	AMIABLE
BRAKE	BROACHED	PURGE	UPBRAID	SPRITE
BASE	BOWER	AUDACIOUS	FILCHED	EXTEMPORE

www.ingramcontent.com/pod-product-compliance
Lightning Source LLC
Chambersburg PA
CBHW081456070526
44586CB00019B/2380